Cambridge Elements

Cambridge Elements in International Economics
edited by
Kenneth A. Reinert
George Mason University

A BEHAVIORAL FINANCE APPROACH TO INTERNATIONAL MONETARY AND FINANCIAL ANALYSIS

Implications and Evidence

Thomas D. Willett
Claremont Graduate University and Claremont McKenna College

CAMBRIDGE
UNIVERSITY PRESS

CAMBRIDGE
UNIVERSITY PRESS

Shaftesbury Road, Cambridge CB2 8EA, United Kingdom

One Liberty Plaza, 20th Floor, New York, NY 10006, USA

477 Williamstown Road, Port Melbourne, VIC 3207, Australia

314–321, 3rd Floor, Plot 3, Splendor Forum, Jasola District Centre, New Delhi – 110025, India

Cambridge University Press is part of Cambridge University Press & Assessment, a department of the University of Cambridge.

We share the University's mission to contribute to society through the pursuit of education, learning and research at the highest international levels of excellence.

www.cambridge.org
Information on this title: www.cambridge.org/9781009694018

DOI: 10.1017/9781009694001

When citing this work, please include a reference to the DOI 10.1017/9781009694001

First published 2026

A catalogue record for this publication is available from the British Library

A Cataloging-in-Publication data record for this Element is available from the Library of Congress

ISBN 978-1-009-69401-8 Hardback
ISBN 978-1-009-69398-1 Paperback
ISSN 2753-9326 (online)
ISSN 2753-9318 (print)

A Behavioral Finance Approach to International Monetary and Financial Analysis

Implications and Evidence

Cambridge Elements in International Economics

DOI: 10.1017/9781009694001
First published online: May 2026

Thomas D. Willett
Claremont Graduate University and Claremont McKenna College

Author for correspondence: Thomas D. Willett, Tom.Willett@cgu.edu

Abstract: Efficient market theory has made an important contribution to economic and financial analysis, but markets do not always behave according to the theory's predictions. The behavioral finance approach advocated in this Element is a complement to efficient market theory. The Element stresses the effects of perverse incentives, complexity, and uncertainty, as well as the roles of mental models or narrative and behavioral biases. It emphasizes limits to arbitrage, suggesting that international capital mobility is often far from perfect. It reviews popular models and considers alternatives in areas such as currency crises, exchange rates and the balance of payments, the international monetary trilemma, capital flow surges and sudden stops, and the discipline effects of international financial markets. The behavioral approach of the Element also helps to explain why governments often fail to undertake necessary policy adjustments in time to head off currency and financial crises.

Keywords: financial analysis, political economy, business economists, policy officials, behavioral finance

ISBNs: 9781009694018 (HB), 9781009693981 (PB), 9781009694001 (OC)
ISSNs: 2753-9326 (online), 2753-9318 (print)

Contents

1 Introduction

Efficient market theory has made an important contribution to economic and financial analysis. It has become clear, however, that markets do not always behave according to its predictions. This has given rise to efforts to help explain why markets do not always behave efficiently. This Element analyzes some of the key implications of taking a broad behavioral finance approach to the study of international monetary and financial analysis.[1] Beyond traditional behavioral finance, it draws on evolutionary and complexity economics and emphasizes the roles of uncertainty and mental models or narratives. It views behavioral finance as a complement to, rather than a substitute for, efficient market theory. While a rich literature on behavioral finance has developed in recent years, there have been relatively few applications of this approach to the areas of international money and finance.

This Element provides an overview of major implications of a behavioral approach to topics such as the degree of international capital mobility and financial integration, models of open economy macroeconomics, currency and financial crises and contagion, capital flow surges and sudden stops, the discipline effects of international financial markets, the international monetary trilemma, and official intervention in foreign exchange markets.

The broad approach presented here is eclectic and emphasizes not only behavioral biases but also the informational and cognitive limitations and perverse incentives such as principal–agent problems that can lead markets to behave inefficiently. This approach also draws on insights from the literature on adaptive markets, bounded rationality, evolutionary and complexity economics, faulty mental models, network theory, agent-based modeling, and the importance of uncertainty emphasized by Keynes and more recently by Kay and King (2020). It also focuses on important interactions among these factors. While these different approaches are sometimes presented as being competitors, I view aspects of them as being largely complementary.[2] There is no name generally in use for approaches that combine elements of all of these, so I have chosen the *broad behavioral approach* label despite its limitations.[3]

This broad behavioral finance approach taken here does not assume that markets always behave irrationally with wild mood swings from euphoria to

[1] The study draws on my earlier papers Willett (2022) and (2024).

[2] In a similar vein, Lo (2019) argues that in complex environments, which often include financial markets, "aspects of psychology, neuroscience, evolutionary biology and artificial intelligence [can be] of critical importance to understanding market behavior" (p. 177). Of course, none of us can be experts in all of these fields but we can draw on the conclusions from such literatures.

[3] It has been suggested that given the range of literature that it draws upon, calling it a cross-disciplinary approach would actually be more accurate. However, since it draws most strongly on behavioral finance, I have chosen to use the label broad behavioral approach.

panic, but does point to aspects of nonrational behavior that sometimes are important.[4] Of course, "irrationality" is a loaded term, frequently associated with wild irrationality.[5] Many of the biased behaviors that have been discovered in cognitive science and applied in behavioral economics and finance are not due to wild irrationality or pathologies but, as Perlmutter, Campbell, and MacCoun (2024) have argued, are "properties of normal human cognition" (p. 173). These can be particularly important under conditions of great uncertainty.

There is not space here to give an adequate review of all of the important contributions of the leading behavioral economics scholars such as Kahneman (2011), Lo (2019), Shleifer (2000), Shiller (2020), and Thaler (2015), and all of the possible applications to the areas of international monetary and financial analysis. What I have tried to do is to give a flavor of the potential contributions by explaining a selected set of their contributions that I have found particularly useful for my own research.[6]

Such considerations suggest that we should not assume that financial markets always behave in the same way. Unlike arguments sometimes made, this broad approach does not reject the usefulness of efficient market theory, but views it as one of a number of valuable perspectives. As Andrew Lo (2019) has argued, the problem with efficient market theory is if it is taken as all-encompassing. In his view, "the Efficient Market Hypothesis isn't wrong, it's just incomplete " (p. 3).

Within the behavioral economics and cognitive psychology literature, many different potential behavioral biases have been identified.[7] For our purposes some are much more important than others. Here I will focus on a limited number of them which I have found to be particularly useful in international monetary and financial analysis.

---

[4] Greenspan (2014) refers to animal spirits tempered by reason to a greater or lesser extent.

[5] As Pinker (2021) states: "What is irrationality? . . . no one definition can stipulate its meaning exactly," (p. 6). Furthermore, the term *irrational* is often taken to mean wild irrationality, while for most of the behavior emphasized here, nonrational would be more descriptive. Thus, in this study I have chosen to refer to biases in decision making. Greenspan (2014) has chosen the term propensities. It could be argued that the use of the term *biases* implies that we know what is rational. In standard economics, it often has a clear meaning in terms of deviations from optimization in the particular economic model being considered. But as Kay and King (2020) argue, we can unambiguously specify rational or efficient decision making only in the context of cases where the issue is well-specified. In situations of complexity and uncertainty standard optimization procedures often do not work well. In such cases irrationality is difficult to assess and reasonable people may differ in their judgments of specific cases. Here I use "biases" in a non-comprehensive sense of the repeated occurrence of behavior that is counter-productive in terms of achieving the agent's objectives. For further discussions of different types or rationality including evolutionary rationality see Kay and King (2020) and Smith (2008).

[6] I do not cover the substantial literature on corporate and household behavioral finance since these are not directly relevant to the international issues that are my focus.

[7] For discussions of many of the most important of these see Kahneman (2011).

Examples of these are hubris, the tendency for normative considerations to color positive analysis, confirmation bias, shortsightedness, and the tendency to put excessive faith in particular narratives or mental models. Such biases are especially important under conditions of complexity and uncertainty.

An important issue is to what extent various biases may offset each other so as not to have major effects in aggregate. For example, the literature in cognitive psychology has identified the possibilities of both underreaction and overreaction to news. If the effects of these opposing tendencies were of roughly equal magnitude, they would largely cancel each other out and lead to an approximation of the efficient market result. Similarly, tendencies for both excessive optimism and excessive pessimism have been found. At times these might largely cancel each other out. On the other hand, in booms overoptimism may predominate, while in busts pessimism might dominate. Another example is that the tendencies of people to be hesitant to sell losers might help reduce the bias toward overtrading. While further theorizing may be helpful, it seems likely that this may not be able to give us a great deal of insight into which biases will dominate when two or more conflict. These are clearly empirical questions. Answering such questions is likely to be particularly difficult because relative strengths are likely to vary in different situations.

While sometimes conflicting, many of the potential biases often act to reinforce each other. For example, contagious overoptimism based in part on the widespread adoption of a common false or seriously exaggerated narrative, especially of the "this time is different" variety, combined with poor memories of previous bubbles and crises, can help create the beginning of a bubble and then interact with herding tendencies and fear of missing out (FOMO) tendencies to keep the bubbles going while confirmation bias leads market participants to pay insufficient attention to warning signals. These various potential biases will be discussed in Section 3.

A key aspect of behavioral finance is that limits to arbitrage can be quite important. Indeed, these limits are essential to the relevance of much of standard behavioral finance because in the absence of such limits, rational speculators would tend to offset the effect of less rational ones. The amount of arbitrage funds is likely to vary considerably across markets, particularly when it is recognized that what is called arbitrage in the finance literature can be quite risky. There is considerable evidence that international capital mobility, while often high, is frequently considerably less than perfect, so that behavioral biases can be important. Such limits to arbitrage have important implications for issues such as the international monetary trilemma and official intervention in the foreign exchange markets.

It should be emphasized that the types of biases considered here are not limited to private sector behavior. Policymakers are often subject to pressures emanating from the public, which are often influenced by similar biases such as short time horizons. Policy officials and regulators themselves are also often subject to such biases. Both private and public sector biases can lead to inefficient policies and can result in major crises. While detailed discussions are beyond the scope of this Element, a number of such cases will be briefly discussed.

We begin with brief reviews of standard behavioral finance and efficient market theory and go on to consider motivations such as perverse incentives, defective mental models, and uncertainty, which can lead to inefficient market outcomes. We then apply insights from these approaches to a wide range of international monetary and financial theories and issues. These include critiques of major international monetary and macroeconomic and currency crisis models and discussion of some of the faulty mental models that have contributed importantly to a wide range of currency and financial crises, such as the Mexican, Asian, and Russian crises in the 1990s and the eurozone and global financial crises in the 2000s.

2 Behavioral Finance and Efficient Market Theory

2.1 Behavioral Finance

Behavioral economists come in two flavors: those who view behavioral considerations as substitutes for traditional economic analysis based on the assumption of rational decision makers and those who view them as complements.[8] I am in the later camp which I believe is now the majority view. This approach needs not only to investigate various possible deviations from efficiency, rational or not, but also the conditions under which different types of behavior are more likely to occur. These will interact with the standard economic rational reasons for inefficient outcomes such as moral hazard and principal–agent problems, which will be discussed in Section 3.

We can identify at least three important complementary strands of a broad-based behavioral approach. The first investigates various possible deviations from the types of rational decision making assumed in most traditional economic analysis and the implications of these various deviations.

[8] A representative group of contributions and texts on behavioral finance include Bhoj (2019), Barberis and Thayler (2002), Bossaerts (2009), Burham (2008), Burton and Sunit (2013), Gennaioli and Shleifer (2018), Ibbotson et al. (2018), Illiashenko (2017), Kahneman (2011), Menschel (2002), Lo (2019), Shiller (2020), Shleifer (2000), Thaler (2015), and Zweig (2007).

The second strand emphasizes real-world constraints such as imperfect information, decision making costs, and limitations to humans' cognitive powers. These can lead to behavior that would be irrational in the context of the standard economic models but can become rational in more complex environments. Kay and King (2020) refer to such considerations as behavior in small versus large worlds. An important early contribution to this approach was Simon's (1991) concept of bounded rationality and this has given rise to large literatures on the economics of information, including the effects of perverse incentive structures such as principal–agent and moral hazard problems.[9] Complexity economics is also an important element of this strand.

One important aspect recently stressed by Kay and King is Knight's (1921) important distinction between risk and uncertainty, also emphasized by Keynes (1921).[10] Much of economics has tended to treat imperfect information as a matter of decision making under risk, where probability distributions are known, even as the particular outcomes from those distributions are not. Kay and King show that this approach can lead to serious difficulties when the true situation is one of uncertainty and the probability is not known. A prime example was putting too much faith in value at risk (VaR) models which lured many financial decision makers into taking on more risk than they realized. The standard VaR models assumed a normal distribution which gives too little weight to tail events such as crises. To relax this assumption, current technologies such as the bootstrap, Monte Carlo methods, and machine learning models involve conducting thousands of resampling calculations to simulate and derive probability distributions which can then be used to calculate VaR. While there have been substantial improvements, these methods are still subject to the problem of structural shifts.

Coping with uncertainty can make behaviors, such as emphasis on narratives, stories, or mental models, and rules of thumb, which would be quite irrational in a world of traditional economic models, rational.[11] The potential for efficient use of simple narratives under conditions of uncertainty has also recently been emphasized by Shiller (2020), as have the problems generated by the spread of false narratives.

Although it can be argued that this approach should not be considered part of the behavioral approach per se, I see it as very kindred in spirit in terms of

[9] See Simon (1991). [10] See also King's (2016) earlier book.

[11] In this study I will use *narratives*, *stories*, and *mental models* interchangeably. Mental models are constructs attempting to focus on key aspects of an issue and how different factors interact. They include, but are not limited to, formal mathematical models. While narratives and stories share these attributes, they often go beyond such positive analysis to include statements about desirable values or preferences. In other words, they can include normative as well as positive elements. The focus in this study, however, is their use as positive guides to how the world works.

helping to explain why simple models of rationality sometimes do not work. Thus, I include it under a broad concept of the behavioral approach. Alternatively, one could consider it as a complementary approach to a narrower concept of behavioral finance.

A third strand of literature has emerged that has begun to look for explanations in terms of evolutionary theory. These writers stress that evolution operates over a long time scale and that many of the habits that cause problems for behavior in financial markets today stem from behavior that was beneficial in the past. Thus, "Homo sapiens haven't had time to adjust to the new realities of life" (Lo 2019, p. 20). The financial sector is an area where the need for adjustment to modern conditions is particularly great. Drawing on recent advances in neuroscience, this approach stresses how the structure of the brain itself limits its ability to instantly adapt. While the evolution of the brain offers new capacities and powers of analysis, this new capacity was built on top of, rather than replacing, our primitive instincts developed at an earlier stage of evolution in the amygdala, sometimes called the "lizard" part of our brain.[12] These two portions of the brain are the basis for Kahneman's important contribution, *Thinking, Fast and Slow* (2011), which stresses the differences between what he calls System 1 and System 2 thinking, one operating quickly based on instincts and the other operating more slowly based on more analytical thought.

Drawing on this type of analysis, Lo (2019) suggests that "investors and financial markets behave more like biology than physics," and that "the principles of evolution are more useful for understanding the inner workings of the financial industry than the physics like principles of rational economic analysis" (p. 2). While the question of which approach is more useful is quite interesting, we need not reach a conclusion on the issue to acknowledge that both are important.

2.2 Efficient Market Theory and Its Critics

There are two major propositions associated with efficient market theory. One is that individual agents cannot beat the market. There are likely exceptions to this conclusion but a looser form – that it is very hard to beat the markets – has a huge amount of support, at least for well-developed financial markets.[13]

The second and much stronger conclusion is that markets quickly set the correct or equilibrium price. While this second conclusion implies the first,

[12] See, for instance, Burham (2008).

[13] Note that this distinction between the two major conclusions of efficient market theory is different from Fama's distinction between the strong and weak forms of the efficient market hypothesis which are based on the types of information available. Most empirical studies of the efficiency of markets focus on the first type.

contrary to what has often been assumed, the first proposition need not imply the second. The considerable evidence supporting the first proposition need not provide equal support for the second one.[14]

A key assumption of efficient markets theory is that there are no serious limits to arbitrage, so that efficient speculators can take advantage of irrational ones and in the process will make profits and force prices to their efficient levels. Only when these arbitrage conditions are not met will the cognitive biases discussed in the behavioral finance literature become relevant for market prices. Even in many well-developed financial markets, these assumptions sometimes do not hold. Many of the opportunities to take advantage of perceived mispricing of assets are in fact quite risky. The current popularity of the label *risk arbitrage* is actually a contradiction in terms since it is not risk-free arbitrage. This label has perhaps become preferred as it sounds more socially acceptable than calling it speculation, which it actually is.[15] We turn next to a discussion of the major types of conditions, both rational and behavioral, why markets may not produce efficient outcomes.

3 Major Impediments to Financial Sector Efficiency

3.1 Reasons Consistent with Rational Behavior

3.1.1 Weak Institutional Infrastructures

In the literatures on industrial organization and economic development, stress is usually put on the infrastructure of markets and their degree of competitiveness. The quality of market infrastructure includes many aspects. Among these are low barriers to entry which allow many participants, the quality of the legal structures which facilitate the enforceability of contracts, the extent of crony capitalism, the quality of regulation and supervision, and political and economic stability.

In terms of international portfolio investments, countries are usually classified as emerging market economies (EMEs) and advanced market countries. Emerging market economies generally are middle-income countries that have made considerable progress in terms of developing stronger institutions and more developed financial markets, but which have still not reached the levels of

[14] An example of the distinction between these two conclusions is given by Burt Malkiel, one of the leading proponents of the first proposition of efficient markets theory but who also argues that at times bubbles do exist and push prices far away from equilibrium levels. See Malkiel (2023).

[15] This distinction is important for the distinction between covered and uncovered arbitrage between currencies. As will be discussed later, CIP tends to hold much more strongly than for uncovered arbitrage.

the advanced economies. The dividing lines between these two categories are not always clear-cut.

In general, the less developed the financial markets, and the lower the underlying quality of institutions and economic and political stability, the greater are the opportunities for profit but also the greater the risks. This is one of the major reasons why more capital tends to flow to EMEs when global risk seems low and less when it is high. The markets often refer to these as conditions of risk on and risk off. While the implication of efficient market theory, that greater returns can be earned only by taking on greater risks, is not always true, it holds often enough to be important for investors to keep in mind.

3.1.2 Perverse Incentives

A key insight of economic analysis is the importance of incentive structures, as evidenced in Adam Smith's concept of the invisible hand, where the pursuit of individual interests leads to outcomes that have socially desirable properties.[16] But as Adam Smith well understood, such desirable outcomes depend on particular conditions holding. Modern economics has placed a good deal of attention on specifying in more detail the conditions under which results are likely to occur and when not. The degree of competition, externalities, and public goods are important considerations. The financial market has been a major area of application of these principles. Many studies have focused on the nature of principal–agent problems within this context.

It is widely, although not universally, recognized that monetary systems display important elements of public goods.[17] Important externalities keep money from managing itself and present a strong case for public government provision of the money supply and some degree of financial regulation.[18] The latter is not only to avoid fraud such as Ponzi schemes but also to offset a host of incentives for excessive risk-taking generated by principal–agent problems and moral hazard. In many cases it is quite difficult to devise compensation schemes for financial institutions that do not give agents incentives for excessive risk-taking. Likewise, the prospect of government bailouts can generate situations where private sector institutions can capture all of their profits but socialize

[16] Smith, 1776.

[17] It is monetary stability and the facilitation of exchange that are the public goods, not money itself.

[18] Some Austrian economists reject these arguments and argue for purely private provision of money. It is possible that this may work when there are only a few large banks, see, for example, White (1989), but the US experiences of numerous financial panics during the 1800s eras of wildcat banking show that this can be a dangerous strategy for general use. Likewise, the global financial crisis of 2007–08 showed that competition alone is not sufficient to promote financial stability. See, for example, Willett (2012).

some of their losses and thus have incentives for excessive risk-taking. This is one of the major arguments for some types of financial regulation. The incentives of fund managers also contribute to tendencies toward herding behavior.[19]

In many industries competition is sufficient to produce incentives for efficient production. Some economists and regulators, most famously Alan Greenspan, believed that competition would both keep costs down in the banking sector, and also promote prudent risk-taking. Sadly, as shown in the US subprime crisis, competition for market share can at times lead to excessive risk-taking, challenging these claims. To his credit, Greenspan did acknowledge that his views of this question had proven to be wrong.[20]

Perverse incentives can also influence policy officials, such as the short time horizons generated by upcoming elections, and the heavy influence of interest groups.

3.1.3 Cognitive Limitations

Humans have an enormous capacity for thinking, but it is not unlimited. Even the brightest individuals have limits to how much and how well they can store and process information. The expansion of information technology such as computers and the web has greatly expanded our abilities, but there are still strong limits, especially with respect to our ability to analyze and draw conclusions from a large number of facts. Simon (1991) drew attention to this issue with his concept of bounded rationality. It is discussed further in Section 5.3.

3.1.4 Complexity Economics

As evidence of irrational overreactions to crises, it is often pointed out that small developments will sometimes have effects vastly out of proportion to their magnitude. Here, a knowledge of the behavior of complex systems can be quite instructive. Tightly coupled systems are often nonlinear, and a failure of a small component can sometimes cause the whole system to crash.[21]

Financial systems can also become tightly coupled as the result of complex systems of lending and borrowing among different institutions in the system.

---

[19] Sadly, poor management can often add to such difficulties. For example, while there is no perfect solution to such principal–agent problems, many managers did not worry about such problems sufficiently. Just as there is a wide range of abilities among athletes there is also a wide range of abilities across managers, even apart from differences in their abilities to counter the various biases discussed in the behavioral literature.

[20] See Greenspan (2014).

[21] An excellent discussion of this type of possibility is given in Bookstaber (2007). See also the broad-ranging discussion of complexity and evolutionary economics in Beinhocker (2007).

Failures with large systemic effects are not limited to the largest financial institutions. Lehman Brothers was one of the smallest of the US investment banks, but it was highly connected with other institutions through a web of investments and lending and borrowing, including highly complex and opaque derivatives. Its failure in 2008 chained through the system to other financial institutions and led to a system-wide crisis. This led to the addition of "too interconnected to fail" to the category of "too big to fail."

A major reason why the effects of the US subprime crises were so much more devastating than those of the dot-com bubble crash was that, in the subprime crisis, the banking sector was much more heavily involved in the financing of real estate than in financing investors, as in the dot-com bubble. High leverage can increase profits, sometimes substantially in good times, but be devastating in bad times. This is why regulators put limits on the degrees of leverage allowed for banks.[22]

Small shocks can have large effects even with all actors behaving rationally. In financial markets, this typically occurs when markets have become too exuberant and have moved into disequilibrium situations, such as during bubbles. In the physical sciences such situations are often referred to as displaying far-from-equilibrium behavior where the system becomes nonlinear and small shocks can generate phase transitions and have large consequences.

3.2 Behavioral Biases

Behavioral biases constitute the area most associated with the technical literature on behavioral and neuroeconomics, and finance. A standard argument often made by economists against those arguing for irrational behavior is that there are almost an infinite number of ways in which people could be irrational, so it is difficult to undertake useful analysis based on this. Developments in cognitive psychology and neuroscience have made this much less of a problem by focusing on a more limited set of possibilities.

The number of such potential biases is quite large, but behavioral economists and finance experts have been able to focus on a limited number that appears likely to be particularly relevant for economic and financial behavior, and which can often be formulated in ways that can be subject to empirical testing. Here I focus on an even smaller set that I have found to be highly useful for international monetary and financial analysis.

---

[22] The subprime crisis also illustrated the importance of looking at gross, not just net, capital flows.

3.2.1 Arbitrary Mood Swings Aren't That Important

When people are asked about behavioral biases, the first things likely to come to mind are mood swings from excessive optimism to excessive pessimism. Sadly, a nontrivial number of people do suffer from what used to be called manic depression and now more politely is referred to by experts as bipolar disorder. It seems doubtful, however, that such individuals are the major cause of large market swings. More likely than pure psychological factors are developments which shift an individual's perceptions from types of mental models with rosy outlooks to ones with pessimistic outlooks.

In most of the crises that I have studied, the panics were largely quite rational, stimulated by events that showed that market actors had been operating under the influence of false mental models and failures to fully appreciate emerging financial difficulties.[23] We will consider a number of examples of this later in this study. In such cases, the primary market failures were not due mainly to excessive panic when the crisis broke out, but rather to the buildup of excessively risky financial positions before the crisis.[24] While there are often some purely psychological factors that influence the magnitudes of crises and the contagion that they generate, more often these effects are quite rational, as individuals discover that positions that they thought were safe are recognized to not be. In the language of the literature, crises in one country or market often act as "wake-up calls" leading investors to reevaluate their financial positions. Such behavior, of course, conflicts with efficient market theory because it implies that prior to the crisis lenders and borrowers were asleep.

3.2.2 Overconfidence, Confirmation Bias, Wishful Thinking, and the Tendency for Normative Views to Color Positive Analysis

One of the most important behavioral biases is the tendency to overrate our abilities, resulting in hubris and overconfidence. Indeed, Kahneman (2011) has suggested that this is perhaps the most important bias. Almost all of us know

[23] Many European banks were highly exposed to the US crisis despite there being little net capital flows from these banks to the US. The European banks had borrowed heavily from US money market funds and invested the funds in asset backed securities. Thus, they were exposed to considerable risk despite only modest net positions.

[24] An important exception is the crash of the US stock market in 1987. This was set off by no major event. Once it started, however, it led to recognition by many that the market had become substantially overvalued. A considerable portion of the initial sharp decline was generated not just by panic but by computer-driven programs based on strategies of so-called portfolio insurance. The problem with such strategies is that while they could be useful for individual investors if they were not a large part of the market, these strategies had become so popular that a large part of the market was guided by these programs. When the market started to fall, there were few buyers that the market crashed.

people who exhibit a great deal of hubris and considerably overstate their superiority over the average person. For example, on a wide range of issues, two-thirds or more of the participants in surveys rate themselves above average.[25] Experts tend to be as subject to such biases as the general public. Many have a tendency to understate the degree of uncertainty about their estimates of different factors.[26] Such overconfidence can lead agents to over-estimate their ability to select the most appropriate mental models, to under-stand various situations, and to pick up new signals more rapidly than others. Often such narratives or mental models are varieties of "this time is different" views. Such people may pay little attention to views other than their own and focus much more on developments that support their initial views than those that conflict.

This tendency is referred to as "confirmation bias." Individuals may tend to give much more weight to developments that are consistent with their views than to those that conflict. This tendency can be quite strong at times with respect to the evidence concerning individuals' mental models or narratives, that is, their positive views of how the world works. In a complex world, people who are quite rational can adopt views that turn out to be wrong. Where irrationality can come in is when too little homework is done in choosing mental models and being too reluctant to change them in the face of the evidence.[27]

3.2.3 Short Memories, High Discount Rates, and Time Inconsistency Problems

Another set of potential biases involve time, both forward and backward looking. One of the most serious contributors to the generation of crises is the tendency during good times to forget crises that occurred before. The caution that usually initially follows crises often tends to decline over time, leading to a gradual relaxation of vigilance and an increase in risk-taking. This seems to be particularly true as new decision makers enter the market who were not directly involved in decision making during the previous crisis. It is much harder to learn from other people's mistakes than from our own.

We can also have problems which involve likely future developments. Short time horizons mean that people do not look far enough ahead with respect to

[25] Of course, we all also know individuals who underrate their abilities, but the surveys show that such people are generally a substantial minority.

[26] In fact, there is evidence that one of the traits of superior forecasters is humbleness.

[27] Of course, it can be quite difficult to figure out how much homework should be undertaken, but there are certainly cases where objective observers could agree that too little effort was made and/or it wasn't implemented in efficient ways.

possible future developments and the longer-run effects of current decisions. Furthermore, even when we do look far enough ahead, we may place too little weight on likely future developments, that is, we apply excessively discounted time rates. This is a particularly strong problem with respect to actions where the time paths of the good and bad effects are quite different. With high discount rates or short time horizons, there will be a tendency to adopt policies whose benefits tend to come early and the costs later.

Rational political incentives such as wishing to be reelected can contribute complementary rational incentives to behave in this way. This can lead to tendencies for excessive credit growth, excessive delays in adopting needed adjustment policies, and the generation of political business cycles, all important causes of currency and financial crises.

3.2.4 Tendencies for Herd Behavior

Tendencies for herd behavior are often seen as one of the most important causes of misbehaving markets. Mood swings can be contagious and can contribute to herding behavior. As noted section 3.2.1, however, my view is that the role of such pure mood shifts, while not irrelevant, is frequently overemphasized. There are many other important reasons for herding, some of them quite rational, particularly in situations of considerable uncertainty.

Humans are social animals, which generates for many the desire to go along with what others are doing. This includes herding in the adoption of narratives or mental models. Herding has important evolutionary roots. Group identity was an important trait for survival in earlier times. It is a prime example of the importance of evolutionary considerations. In the plains of Africa, a movement in the high grass could be due either to the wind or to a lion, but the cost of falsely assuming it was the wind was far greater than the cost of not running when it was indeed a lion.

With imperfect information there can be quite rational reasons to herd. The rationality of doing this in particular circumstances will depend in part on the relative costs of type 1 and type 2 errors. For example, if you hear stories that your bank may be in trouble, the cost of pulling out your uninsured deposits when it proved to be a false rumor are far less than the cost of leaving your money in and later finding out that the rumor was true. Likewise, often the costs of moving your money out of a currency in the face of rumors of a possible crisis are much lower than the costs of staying in when a crisis actually occurs.[28]

[28] Differences in the costs of mistakes are one of the major reasons why the private markets are often much quicker to respond to emerging problems than are governments.

Furthermore, as Lo emphasizes, quite commonly individual managers' performance is compared with those of other managers, so they are likely to be penalized when their more accurate perceptions of risks lead them to make more conservative and, in consequence, less profitable investments during the boom period, while the less conservative managers tend to face lower penalties when the greater risks actually show up because most of the other managers are suffering similar losses. This presents a strong incentive for investment managers to herd and illustrates how perverse incentives can interact with psychological biases.

3.2.5 Blame Avoidance

The desire to save face and not look wrong is one of the strongest human motivations (see Perlmutter et al. 2024). Thus, many people have a strong hesitancy to not admit that they were wrong. In some cases, this is quite rational, for example, to keep one's job or bonus or to avoid bad publicity. For example, the desire to avoid blame is likely an important factor in why the IMF sometimes continues to lend to countries that have failed to undertake sufficient adjustment to adequately deal with their balance of payments problems. They generally get little pushback from overlending, compared with what they will get if they fail to lend and there is a crisis. Domestic politicians likewise tend to blame the IMF for requiring painful but necessary domestic economic adjustments. However, the extent and success of this scapegoating function of the IMF has been the subject of some controversy. See, for example, Kern et al. (2019).

Apart from external appearances, many people find it difficult to admit mistakes to themselves. This is important in helping to explain the differences in interpretations of the causes of previous crises. For example, those on the left have tended to blame the US subprime crisis on greed and financial deregulation, while many on the right viewed government effort to increase home ownership and excessively lower credit standards as the main cause.[29] This is an important example of confirmation bias and of the tendency for normative desires to distort positive analysis.

3.3 Faulty Mental Models

A frequent cause of market failures such as bubbles, crashes, and currency and financial crises is the widespread adoption by market actors of narratives or

[29] The crisis was the result of the interaction of many factors, some of them highly important and others less so. Thus, with crises it is almost always possible to point to one or more of one's own pet views as having been a factor.

mental models which turn out to be faulty.[30] The world can be complex, so it is not necessarily a sign of irrationality that people sometimes hold views that turn out to be incorrect. However, potential irrationality may appear under circumstances such as the following:

- Doing insufficient homework before adopting a particular view, especially as a result of going with the herd and adopting fashionable narratives such as "this time is really different";
- Adopting a narrative because one would like it to be true, an example of wishful thinking and confusing positive with normative analysis;
- Placing excessive faith in a particular narrative to the exclusion of considering other possibilities. Potential causes for this are hubris, leading to the belief that those with other views aren't as smart and just don't "get it," and confusing views that do have some explanatory power with thinking that they are all that is relevant;
- Excessively discounting evidence that contradicts one's view, confirmation bias.

It is sometimes difficult to decide unambiguously whether sufficient analysis has gone into the selection of a particular narrative or mental model. Likewise, it is often impossible to take every potential contingency into account when making decisions. There are questions about which reasonable people may often differ in particular cases. As has been pointed out by authors such as Kay and King (2020), rationality is difficult to apply to narratives. They suggest it is more useful to use concepts such as "productive" or "counter-productive," or from an evolutionary perspective, adaptive or maladaptive.

As with formal theories, it is important to distinguish between narratives that are fundamentally wrong and those which are accurate yet leave out major aspects of the question. It is usually impossible to take every aspect and potential contingency into account when making decisions. Thus, few theories can be complete. Faulty decision making comes in where agents treat the story as if what it focuses on are the only things that matter. This tendency becomes particularly counterproductive when the narrative selected focuses only on a minor, rather than major, aspect of the issue.

Given the lack of objective criteria to label particular narratives as faulty, I leave it to the readers to make their own judgments about particular narratives. In the following section I briefly discuss a series of major financial crises where faulty narratives or mental models contributed importantly to the crisis.

[30] See, for example, Shiller (2020) and Willett (2012).

4 Examples of Faulty Mental Models Contributing to Major Crises

The following are all examples of cases where faulty mental models made important contributions to major crises. Seldom if ever do faulty narratives give a complete explanation of crises. They typically interact with other factors to make crises more likely and/or worse when they do occur. They can contribute both to factors that create inconsistencies among fundamentals, which are the primary causes of crises, and to factors that contribute to the lack of the early detection of these inconsistencies. This failure to detect inconsistencies allows them to go on longer and increase in magnitude, exacerbating the effects of the crisis when it does break out. While a consensus often develops among researchers about the major causes of a crisis, there is often much less agreement about their relative importance. This is made more difficult by important interactions among these major factors. Examples of such interactions are offered in Section 5.

Closely related to faulty mental models is the simple failure to note plausible possible developments. This was the case with the severe crisis of several regional US banks, starting with Silicon Valley Bank in March 2023. Interest rates had been low for years, so a number of banks invested heavily in long-term Treasury securities without paying attention to the possibility that interest rate increases could greatly reduce the value of these securities.

The bank regulators also ignored this risk in the stress tests they had the banks carry out. When interest rates did begin to rise substantially, this generated large declines in the market value of these securities, threatening bankruptcy and leading to huge outflows of funds. While we could call this the failure of a faulty narrative that interest rates would remain low indefinitely, this was not a major focus of discussions in the same way that the belief that average housing prices could not fall was before the US subprime crisis.

We now turn to brief discussions of some examples of faulty mental models and their contributions to major financial crises.[31]

[31] Two other important false narratives that we do not have space to cover here were Turkey's President Recap Erdogan's argument, contrary to all mainstream economic theory and evidence, that cutting rather than raising interest rates was the way to deal with Turkey's rising inflation in the early 2020s. This led him to fire the mainstream economic advisers and central bank officials who opposed his ideas. Brute facts eventually forced him to abandon this strategy, but only after the Turkish lira had suffered repeated crises and the inflation rate had accelerated to over 75 percent. A second example is Mr. Trump's false belief that trade deficits are always bad which has led to huge increases in US tariffs.

4.1 Kernel of Truth: The Laffer Curve and the UK Crisis

"Kernel of truth" fallacies are true narratives which are carried too far. For example, in stock market bubbles, arguments that "this time Is different" often have some truth, in the sense that the developments which spark them will differ at least somewhat from the innovations that sparked past bubbles, but this does not mean that everything is different, as investors frequently find out when the bubble crashes. One of the most important of these involves the Laffer curve.

In this example, the perfectly valid argument that tax increases will tend to reduce supply was taken too far and transformed into the belief that tax cuts would increase supply so much that they would pay for themselves. Just as there are revenue maximizing prices for firms, there will be revenue maximizing level of taxes and tariffs. When prices or taxes are above these levels, reducing them will increase revenues.

This is a perfectly sound economic concept but has frequently been misused in the political arena. Conservatives had traditionally been viewed as facing a dilemma between their objectives of cutting taxes and avoiding large fiscal deficits. Economist Art Laffer famously introduced the idea into American politics that cutting taxes would increase rather than reduce revenues and hence reduce fiscal deficits, thus offering a way out of the Republican dilemma. While this idea was already well known by economists, it became widely known as the Laffer curve and was quickly embraced by Republicans.

Where there are cases where cutting specific taxes has increased revenue, these were generally cases where supply curves were quite elastic. However, supply schedules for broad-based changes such as income taxes will tend to be much less elastic. Several presidents, most famously Mr. Reagan, tried this strategy, but their income tax cuts did not increase revenues.[32]

This, however, did not keep President Trump from ignoring the evidence and pushing through an income tax cut which he claimed would pay for itself. It did not, and the US deficit soared. Undeterred, President Trump continued to pursue large tax cuts in his second term despite the already huge fiscal deficits. The only surprising thing about this episode is that, while many economists worried about the sustainability of these budget deficits, the financial markets have shown only moderate concern.[33]

However, this was not the case with the budget proposals of the UK's new prime minister Liz Truss in September 2022. Despite all of the accumulated evidence that tax cuts of the levels seen in the US and UK would not pay for themselves, with the UK already in a dire fiscal position, she went ahead and

[32] For further analysis see Auerbach (2018), Bird (2018), and Chodorow-Reich et al. (2024).

[33] On debt sustainability, see the analysis and references in Schuknecht (2022).

proposed a Laffer curve type budget with substantial tax cuts. Given her previous economic writings, it seems entirely possible that she truly believed in the Laffer curve and had not really looked at or not been convinced by the evidence that the cuts would not pay for themselves. In any event, reactions in both the long-term financial and foreign exchange markets were swift and powerful. Many financial institutions had not hedged against possible increases in interest rates, and the substantial increases in rates following Truss's proposal threatened the solvency of many of them. A full-scale financial crisis was a real possibility and forced Truss to withdraw her proposal, after which the markets fairly rapidly calmed and soon after she was forced to resign.

4.2 The False Belief That if the Macro Fundaments Are Sound, Then the Financial and External Sectors Will Take Care of Themselves

4.2.1 The Mexican Crisis

In Mexico, a new reform government with a strong economic team brought the huge fiscal deficit under control and brought inflation down from triple to single digit levels by early 1995. What was largely missed by the market was that while there had been drastic reductions in Mexico's inflation, it was still running higher than in the US, and its crawling peg was depreciating too slowly to keep up with the remaining inflation differential.[34] As a result, Mexico developed a huge current account deficit. Because of large capital inflows there was no trouble initially financing this huge deficit, and for a time Mexico actually ran a balance of payments surplus. Fairly soon, however, the capital inflows began to fall off. Given the huge size of the current account deficit that needed financing, it was unlikely that capital inflows of the size needed to do this would continue indefinitely. The triggers that set off a sharp reversal were growing signs of domestic political instability and a tightening of US monetary policy. A full-fledged crisis soon followed in 1996–97.

4.2.2 The Asian Crisis

In Asia, rapid growth, low inflation, and strong fiscal positions led to large capital inflows into a number of what proved to be the crisis countries known as the "Asian miracle."[35] One of the major faulty mental models was the belief that

[34] A similar oversight contributed to the Italian crisis in the European monetary system in the early 1990s. After joining the system, Italy's inflation rate fell substantially and as a consequence initially attracted considerable capital inflows. What the market seems to have missed was that Italy's slowed inflation was still higher than Germany's, so that the real value of its currency continually appreciated, leading to serious overvaluation.

[35] For an analysis of the Asian crisis see Willett et al. (2004) and the references cited there.

if domestic macroeconomic fundamentals were strong, the foreign exchange and financial markets would take care of themselves. Capital flows surged in, paying little attention to the increasingly overvalued Thai baht and serious financial sector problems in a number of the countries in 1997–98. The later omission can be explained in part by the difficulties of gaining good information in a timely manner about the shape of financial sectors, while the statistics on the strong domestic economic fundamentals were easily obtainable.

A second faulty narrative that strongly affected the financial policies of a number of EMEs was the idea that any type of financial liberalization was good, regardless of the underlying conditions. We know from the theory of the second best that where there are many distortions, removing the distortion in one area can sometimes worsen the overall situation. A prime example is that where there are incentives for financial institutions to take on too much risk because of factors such as being too big or too politically important to fail, then liberalizing the range and quantities of permissible investments can increase the quantities of risky investments undertaken. Likewise, when there is poor regulation and supervision, financial liberalization is often associated with financial crises, whereas this relationship does not tend to hold where there is strong oversight.[36]

4.2.3 The US Subprime Crisis

Several false ideas contributed importantly to the generation of the US subprime crisis of 2007–08. It became widely believed, including by many experts, that average housing prices across the US would not fall. This lay behind the rush to invest in housing both directly and indirectly through various types of mortgage-backed securities. The belief that modern risk management techniques had largely conquered risks led to the popularity of opaque asset-backed securities with ratings that greatly understated their true risks, and a widespread tendency of the financial system toward excessive risk-taking.[37] Confirmation bias also contributed significantly to the failure to pick up on numerous indications of increasing financial fragility.

Monetary officials and financial regulators provided little oversight, again based on the assumption that if macroeconomic fundamentals were sound, the

[36] See Angiknand et al. (2010).

[37] On the contributions of these false mental models to the generation of the US subprime crisis, see the analysis and references in Willett (2012). Among the many articles and books on the crisis, one of the best is Davies (2010), who discusses many different explanations that have been offered. See also Lo's (2012) excellent review of a number of books on the crisis. While there has certainly been learning from the crisis, this has been limited by the degree to which interpretations have been biased based on individual's prior views, a prime example of confirmation bias and normative views coloring positive analysis.

financial system and balance of payments would take care of themselves.[38] Little attention was paid to the failure of this view in the case of Asia. This was also an important contributor to the later euro crisis. Failures in learning will be discussed in the section on learning and forgetting. In the US, this false belief was aided by the conviction of some efficient market advocates, especially Fed Chairman Alan Greenspan, that competition would be sufficient to lead financial institutions to follow prudent risk policies.[39] Instead, it turned out that, among the large financial institutions, the fight for larger market share contributed to the excessive risk-taking.

4.2.4 The Design of the Euro System

The creation of the euro in 1999 provides another important example of excessive focus on macroeconomic fundamentals to the exclusion of financial sector considerations. To convince conservative Germany to join the euro, it was necessary for the other countries to agree to the establishment of a conservative independent central bank to keep inflation low and enforce fiscal limitations to avoid large budget deficits. This arrangement was highly successful in keeping inflation low, although it was less successful with regard to the fiscal agreements, as illustrated by the Greek fiscal crisis of 2009. The belief that any fiscal problems in Greece would be dealt with by the other euro countries led to premia on Greek debt that were almost as low as Germany's, attracting large capital inflows to fund the fiscal deficit. Also of importance in generating the spread of the crisis triggered by Greece was overlending to the real estate sector by financial institutions in many of the European countries, similar to the conditions preceding the subprime crisis in the US. In many of the countries, the widespread bailout of financial institutions then substantially weakened domestic fiscal situations, further contributing to the spread of the crises. Perhaps thc most dramatic example involved Ireland, where a huge real estate boom was facilitated by loose credit from institutions throughout the euro zone. Ireland had an extremely strong fiscal position before the outbreak of the crisis, but the size of the holes in the balance sheets of Ireland's major financial institutions turned out to be much larger than had been thought. This led to the creation of a fiscal deficit equal to almost one-third of Ireland's GDP in 2008.[40]

---

38 While this view is consistent with efficient market theory, it was held at times as far back as the 1920s and contributed importantly to the failure of the Federal Reserve to take actions as the stock market surged. Indeed, the Fed actually cut interest rates in 1927. See the discussion in Sharma (2024).

39 See Greenspan (2014). Advocates of this view would not argue that there was no need for government ground rules, nor would they agree on the optimal degree of regulation, but they would all agree that regulation should be "light touch" rather than extensive.

40 The willingness of the Irish government to guarantee the obligations of its banks was due in part to estimates by both the banks and the financial regulators that the holes in their balance sheets were quite small relative to what turned out to be the actual situation.

4.3 "Countries Don't Go Broke," and the Latin American Debt Crisis

This adage, strongly associated with former head of Citibank Walter Wriston, became popular in the 1970s, and belief in it likely played an important role in generating the flood of bank lending to Latin American governments during that period. On the face of it, Wriston's statement is technically true. As he explained, a country's assets include all of its resources, and these are bound to exceed its international liabilities. These resources do not go away, so countries cannot go out of business as firms would when they become insolvent. Governments do not have all of these resources at their disposal, however, so their assets can frequently fall far below their liabilities. Up to a point this is not a problem, but continued large deficits can lead to debt levels that become unsustainable. History is littered with examples of government defaults, and this is just what happened with a number of Latin American governments, beginning in 1982, and leading to a major threat to the solvency of the US banking system and to a lost decade of growth in Latin America.[41] Heavy initial borrowing may have been quite rational since interest rates were quite low. However, many of the loans were denominated in dollars at variable interest rates, and when US interest rates began to rise substantially, the burdens of these debts increased in step.[42] At the same time there were major slumps in the prices of the major commodities that many of these countries exported. The crises soon followed.

4.4 Moral Hazard and Countries and Institutions Too Important to Default

We are perhaps most used to hearing arguments about moral hazard in the case of private sector institutions that governments consider too economically or politically important to allow them to go bankrupt. These situations can indeed contribute to excessively risky activities, given the assumption that the companies or individuals will keep any profits generated but will be protected at

[41] The US banking system survived due in considerable part to government efforts to extend and pretend, a common feature also with the European financial crisis. While such policies avoided implosions of the banking systems, they also resulted in stretching out the crises much longer than was necessary.

[42] Substantial interest rate increases were also a major cause of the regional bank crisis in the US in 2003. Several of these mid-sized banks had invested heavily in securities when interest rates were low and when they began to raise mark-to-market requirements this resulted in large accounting loses. This in turn helped spark the run on these banks.

least to some degree if things go bad. Such policies can result in perverse liberalization, where connected firms are given more profit opportunities but feel protected against many of the risks they take. Such considerations were quite important in causing the financial sector problems which contributed to the Asian crisis.

In other cases, large amounts of private sector lending to governments were motivated by the belief that, for a variety of reasons, these countries were considered too important by members of the international community to be allowed to default. Such considerations also gave rise to considerable lending by international institutions when troubles began to arise. In a number of cases, however, such official lending served only to postpone, not avoid, defaults. Three of these cases are briefly discussed in the following sub sections.

4.4.1 The Russian Default

A major example in the late 1990s was the unanticipated default of Russia on its external debt. This occurred not long after the breakup of the Soviet Union. The Western countries had made it a major part of their foreign policy statements to help Russia stabilize and liberalize.[43] Even though the Russian government's finances were in bad shape, it was widely assumed by private investors that Russian government debt was implicitly backed by the IMF and Western governments. Indeed, it was widely recognized that the Russian balance of payments was in severe difficulties, caused in part by the decline in oil prices associated with the Asian crisis. This was sometimes referred to as the moral hazard play.

This assumption, while quite plausible, turned out to be wrong. A substantial devaluation of the ruble was widely expected, but default was not. It was generally recognized that the Russian balance of payments was in severe difficulty. Expectations of a large depreciation of the ruble were reflected in the extremely high interest rates on ruble denominated debt. The spark that generated the crisis was the failure of the Russian Duma, its main legislative body, to pass a bill associated with a newly negotiated package of support from the IMF which had strong requirements for fiscal tightening. Pressure from the Western governments had pushed the IMF to bend its rules about lending in cases where solvency was a serious issue, but it could only be pushed so far. With the Duma's negative vote, hopes for an agreement with the IMF were dashed, and money rushed for the exits. The Russian government's decision to

[43] Sadly, these governments were not willing to back up these statements with large levels of funding.

default on its foreign currency debt was not expected, and thus generated considerable contagion in financial markets across the globe, although few actual currency crises occurred.

4.4.2 Argentina

Another case where expectations that a country was too important to be allowed to default was Argentina in the 1990s. After a horrible record of extremely high inflation, a new government adopted a currency board, resulting in a rapid decline in inflation and stimulating large capital inflows. Difficulties began to mount, however, due to the inability of the central government to rein in the substantial fiscal deficits of the regional governments. As with Mexico, respect for the abilities of the new economic team and the impressive record of inflation control may well have led many investors to engage in excessive optimism. A key factor for the continuing large capital inflows was widespread recognition of the US' geopolitical interest in supporting the Argentine government. The US placed considerable pressure on the IMF to continue lending to the government, even after they frequently missed agreed policy targets. The IMF's policy conditionality proved to have quite limited effectiveness.

It is hard to judge the relative importance of the different factors that kept the money rolling into Argentina, but the continued financial support from the IMF, despite its limited effectiveness in imposing policy conditionality, likely played an important role in convincing private investors that it was safe to keep investing. As in the case of Russia, continued political pressure from the US contributed to IMF management's willingness to overlook its own rules, which specified that lending could occur only when there was a reasonable chance that the loans would be repaid. Long before the crisis broke out, economists at the IMF's research department, being less concerned with political pressures, argued that the IMF was throwing good money after bad.

In addition to its ongoing fiscal problems, the US dollar, to which Argentina was fixed, began to appreciate substantially. Relatively little of Argentina's trade was with the US, so the appreciation of the dollar led to substantial overvaluation of Argentina's currency against most of its trading partners. The resulting balance of payments deficit forced monetary contraction and generated a major recession which in turn led to default and abandonment of the currency board.

The market's initial narrative, that the US and the IMF would give Argentina considerable financial support, was correct. However, this support did not prove to be unlimited, and the crisis was only delayed, not avoided.

4.4.3 The Greek Fiscal Crisis

The last example offered here of a fiscally related narrative that turned out to be false concerns the Greek crisis that began in 2009. Greece had a long record of poor economic management before it joined the euro. However, the requirements for entry had led to improved policy, and optimism boomed. Large amounts of capital flowed in to take advantage of the improved economic policies and conditions. Despite considerable persistent fiscal deficits, the risk premia on Greek debt fell drastically to levels only a little above the interest rates on German government debt. Despite the explicit statement in the treaty establishing the euro that bailouts of member governments' debts were prohibited, it became widely assumed that the other euro countries could be relied upon to make Greek government debt almost as safe as German debt.

The markets had also not recognized the huge size of the Greek fiscal deficits until a new government revealed that the previous government had been using various accounting tricks to hide much of the deficit. Risk premia suddenly shot up drastically. However, the assumption that the euro governments viewed Greece as being too important to fail turned out to be partially correct, to the extent that the richer euro countries and the European Central Bank did go to great lengths to avoid Greek default. This was motivated in part by both concerns for the solvency of some of their major financial institutions that had lent substantial sums to Greece, and by fears of the possibility that Greece would drop out of the euro.

Unfortunately, officials were subject to a number of the psychological biases emphasized by behavioral scientists, such as wishful thinking, confirmation bias, and confusing normative with positive analysis. Private sector actors fell prey to the same. As with Argentina, for a long while the major governments and euro zone institutions failed to face up the magnitude of the problem, and kept pretending that a default was not necessary. Sadly, these "extend and pretend" or "kick the can down the road" policies, as they were frequently called by nonofficial commentators, succeeded mostly in allowing the crisis to continue much longer than necessary, with the devastating consequences that the magnitude of the crisis became much bigger. When the governments finally faced up to the full extent of the problem, the restructuring of the Greek debt left the creditors with only about 25 percent of their initial investments.

5 Some Examples of the Interactions Among Biases

While some potential biases tend to offset each other, such as the rationales for markets to both overreact and underreact to news, many more tend to reinforce each other. In this section, we consider several important examples of such reinforcement effects.

5.1 The Interrelationships between Uncertainty and the Prevalence of Behavioral Biases

Under conditions of uncertainty, it is usually much more difficult to tell which narratives or mental models are more appropriate. As Lo (2019) stressed in his adaptive markets hypothesis, markets tend to learn over time, and in stable environments will also tend toward efficiency. But changing environments generate uncertainty, and learning behavior may need to begin all over again, with the added complication of first requiring some unlearning.

Rapid, unambiguous feedback, as well as open minds are both conducive to learning. These conditions apply in many areas, but often not in financial markets. There can be considerable periods of time between some decisions and their consequences. In the meantime, individuals may continue to stick with their initial views. In a complex world, unforeseen developments can make decisions which were ex ante efficient turn out to be ex post inefficient. In complex situations, extracting the signal from the noise can often be a highly difficult and sometimes impossible task.

Given the strong reluctance of many people to admit mistakes, it is often not difficult to convince ourselves, and perhaps also others, that we made the correct decisions ex ante and that our mental models or views of the world remain sound. Hindsight bias can be an important contributor to this process, as can hubris, confirmation bias, and wishful thinking. Some people are so committed to ideas that almost no evidence can convince them that they are wrong. The continued adherence by some to the Laffer curve argument that income tax cuts will pay for themselves remains a major plank of Republican thinking in the US, despite considerable evidence against it.

5.2 Estimating Risk and the Cost of Errors

Important examples of how psychological tendencies or biases may sometimes interact involve the incentives for herding into investment opportunities and excessive responses to lower interest rates. Let us consider first the tendency of investment managers to herd into taking excessively risky investments. Of course, one possible and not completely rational psychological reason for following the leader is the feeling of wanting to belong, a desire which has been ingrained in humans over the ages. A second type is the inheritance of behavior which was quite rational in a previous environment that no longer obtains. In the state of nature in which humans lived for eons, the cost of not following a suddenly running group member could be death by being eaten by a tiger, while the comparative costs of running in response to a false signal was relatively low. What was highly adaptive in that environment may not be so in the environment of today's financial markets.

There are also strictly rational reasons for such responses today, in an environment which itself has important inefficiencies. As Kahneman (2011) discusses, overconfidence in one's forecasting ability often encourages individuals to underestimate risks, and this applies to professional experts as well as amateurs. Indeed, he reports on studies finding that excessive risk-taking in the financial sector is generated more by underestimating risks than by decision makers being overconfident of expected returns, or by the incentives generated by playing with other people's money. While professionals in many fields often tend to substantially understate the likely range of possible outcomes, those who are more accurate about the risks involved, instead of being rewarded for having more accurate forecasts, tend to find themselves replaced by more confident individuals even though their greater apparent confidence is not justified.

An important contributor to such behavior is another possible bias, the tendency to have short time horizons, that is, high rates of time discount. Rewards and punishments often tend to be handed out over fairly short time periods, so that the conservative manager may not still be around when they are proved to be right. There are many stories of risk managers who warned of the greater risks being accumulated by many financial institutions leading up to the US subprime crisis being shunted aside or being replaced. This is a case where more rational individuals tend to lose out because of the environment generated by the less rational behavior of others. And, of course, confirmation bias makes these other actors less likely to pick up on information that support the views of the less overconfident actors.

At first glance, such a tendency of excessive risk-taking would seem to conflict with the emphasis placed by Kahneman and others on the importance of risk aversion. This would seem to yield high risk aversion and, if anything, lead managers to exaggerate the risk of large losses such as typically occur in crises. Behavioral science's emphasis on the importance of framing may help explain this seeming contradiction. For an individual investor in isolation, this would indeed be a contradiction if it were not for the tendency to underestimate risks, which could have a stronger effect. However, where a manager's reputation and financial rewards are heavily influenced by the behavior of others in his "tribe," loss aversion may contribute to going along with the herd. In this framing, the most relevant loss, in this case, is the manager's reputation and perhaps job.[44]

5.3 Learning and Forgetting and Time inconsistency Problems

A central insight of Lo's (2019) adaptive markets hypothesis is that while market participants are subject to the types of biases and cognitive limitations emphasized in the traditional literature on cognitive psychology and behavioral finance, such behavior occurs particularly strongly in rapidly shifting environments where there is great uncertainty. As discussed Section 3.1.3, such environments make it easy for behavioral biases and faulty mental models to thrive. With stable environments there tend to be more consistent feedback from actions. It helps a great deal if such feedback occurs fairly quickly, and the interpretation is unambiguous. It also helps to evaluate the effects of actions if they occur fairly frequently so that there are more data points. Of course, confirmation bias can substantially impede learning. Still, if the environment stays stable long enough, market behavior should tend to evolve toward efficiency. However, as Lo stresses, environments can change frequently so that steady progress toward greater efficiency is not assured.[45]

Learning that old narratives have become defective in the new environment, and that developing new more productive ones is necessary, is what Lo means by evolution at the speed of thought, as opposed to the slow operation of physical evolution. While Lo is fairly optimistic that good narratives will tend to drive out bad ones, Shiller (2020) is much less so. We would expect that narratives about trading strategies would be subject to more useful feedback than those concerning the effects of many types of loans and government policies.[46] It took quite a long time for the results of the risky lending and

[44] Another type of behavior emphasized by Kahneman (2011) is the importance of reference rates. If returns fall in the home country, this presents a new risk return trade-off to the investment manager, and they may quite rationally shift a part of their portfolio toward higher risk investments. This tendency may be pushed beyond efficient levels, however. Where the relevant reference rate is a target rate of return, then to keep up that expected rate of return, a much greater shift into riskier investments would likely be required. This phenomenon may help account for the high degree of responsiveness of investment flows to emerging markets to changes in financial conditions in the advanced economies. Of course, any tendencies to herd would increase the magnitude of responses.

[45] An important topic for further research is to attempt to operationalize the concept of changing environments for decision making in different types of areas and to see if we can develop markers of when environments change enough to warrant changing our mental models or narratives and modes of operation.

[46] Financial narratives tend to evolve more quickly and drive out defective alternatives sooner than political and social narratives. One likely reason that Lo (2019) and Shiller (2020) differ in their degree of optimism about learning is that Shiller spends more time dealing with the later types of narratives.

investments during the housing bubble in the US to demonstrate their true riskiness. Likewise, riding up a bubble can give good feedback until it bursts.

Government policies are also likely to be subject to weak feedback systems. Policies often change only infrequently, yielding fewer data points, and their effects frequently take many years to be fully felt. And even then, interpretations may differ greatly.

Memory can be an important source of learning. Unfortunately, people tend to learn much more from their own mistakes than from those of others. For example, Asian countries tended to learn much more from the Asian crisis of 1997–98 than did the advanced economies, and many of the mistakes leading to the Asian crisis were repeated in the run-up to the global financial crisis in the 2000s.

Agents often give too little weight to likely future developments if they are not expected to occur fairly quickly, as people often have excessively short time horizons, that is, too high time rates of discount. This contributes importantly to another major source of crises, time inconsistency problems. These occur where the effects of the costs and benefits of actions occur disproportionately at different times. People then tend to be excessively biased toward actions that have most of their good effects first and bad effects later, and against actions that have more of their bad effects first and good effects later.

This gives rise to the famous case of political business cycles where, to increase their chances of reelection, governments adopt expansionary policies shortly before elections to benefit from the initial predominantly good effects on output and unemployment, while the bad effects on inflation appear mainly after the election is safely over. Such actions by governments may be quite rational, but to be successful, they rely on the majority of the public not having sufficient information or rational expectations to anticipate the later bad effects. Some new classical economists argued that political business cycles would not be a continuing problem because the public would catch on and punish governments who tried it.

This learning mechanism has often been weak. Memories may be short. Furthermore, such ignorance may be quite rational. In a complex world, it does not pay for voters to be highly informed on a vast range of issues; thus "rational ignorance" is an important concept for political economy analysis. This is overlooked by some proponents of rational expectations macro models, leading to assumptions of much better knowledge than many economic agents actually have. This can, in turn, lead to the conclusion that most changes in policies are anticipated and hence have little impact on the real economy, and that there are only very limited incentives for politicians to generate political business cycles.[47] In the financial sectors, many decision makers have much stronger incentives to be well informed but even there it is often argued that financial markets frequently operate on the basis of excessively short time horizons.

Such time inconsistency problems can also contribute to tendencies for governments to be too slow to adopt anti-inflation policies and undertake timely adjustments to avoid currency and financial crises. Such policies are usually costly in the short run while the benefits occur later, and there is always the chance that future developments would reverse balance of payments deficits. The combination of uncertainty about whether the crisis would actually occur if strong actions are not taken and wishful thinking can be powerful forces leading to failure to take adjustment actions in a timely fashion. Such tendencies will be reinforced if an election is nearing.

In some cases, the meaning of stable environments can be unclear. Take for example the insightful adage associated with Herman Minsky (1975, 1986), among others, that crises are bred in the good times that proceed them. From a shorter-term perspective, the environments of good times and crisis times differ dramatically. But from a longer-term perspective, the tendency of good times to end in crises may be fairly stable in the sense that these are frequently recurring patterns. The time horizons of actors become quite important here. With long memories and foresight, participants in the financial sector, including regulators, should catch on to this pattern and take actions to avoid it. For example, very low volatility might be taken as a signal that the markets are becoming dangerously complacent, rather than that risk is very low.

On the other hand, with short time horizons looking both forward and backward, risks may begin to be substantially underestimated based on recent developments – the "recency" bias explored in behavioral finance. While one major problem with human decision making is the tendency to be shortsighted, also important is the tendency to have short memories. Furthermore, there is a tendency to learn more from one's own mistakes than from those of others, as when the countries hit by the Asian crisis in the late 1990s tended to learn that strong macroeconomic conditions are not sufficient to avoid financial sector problems and engaged in a great deal of productive financial sector reforms, while this episode had much less impact on those in the advanced economies. These lessons became widely recognized only in the wake of the global financial crisis of 2008.

A further problem is that feedback can be ambiguous. Again, the 2008 crisis provides a cogent example. After almost twenty years, the major causes of the

[47] See, for example, the analysis and references in Willett (1988).

crisis are still under debate. While there is a consensus among mainstream economic and financial experts about some of the most important lessons, for example, the limitations of standard value-at-risk models of risk management and the dangers of complicated derivatives that do reduce risk in good times but multiply them during crises, there is still considerable disagreement among many of the far right and left who, consistent with powerful confirmation biases and the coloring of positive analysis by normative considerations, tend to place major blame alternatively on government policies to increase home ownership among lower income families versus the deregulation of financial markets.

6 Some Applications to International Monetary and Financial Questions

6.1 Bubbles and Capital Flow Surges

Domestic asset market bubbles, credit booms, and capital flow surges are natural areas for behavioral analysis. However, contrary to those who view markets as wildly irrational, seldom if ever do these processes start from purely psychological factors. They typically start for good reasons, such as the development of new technologies, an improving economy, or economic reforms in developing countries.

They are almost always aided by easy money. As Vivek Moorthy has pithily put it in private correspondence, "strict credit limits can curb animal spirits." Monetary and financial officials often fall prey to the same types of overoptimism that can plague the private sector. The faulty mental model discussed earlier, that if inflation is low the financial sector will take care of itself, also often plays a major role in causing monetary and financial officials to play an enabling role in the generation and continuance of bubbles and capital flow surges through the provision of easy credit.

The problem is that these initially rational reactions sometimes take on a life of their own. The initial success of investments based on recognition of these new developments can become self-propelled by a host of behavioral factors. One is the tendency for false extrapolation. Despite the standard warnings from financial institutions that past performance is no guarantee of future performance, for some individuals, recent substantial price increases can lead to expectations that they will continue, attracting more investors in the markets and increasing both the demand for loans and the willingness of financial institutions to supply them. Wishful thinking can be important here since investors would like the price increases to continue.

Especially with respect to asset prices, stories or narratives may start to spread that such price increases can continue for long periods because "this time is different." Old criteria for evaluating equilibrium prices are no longer relevant. Those who urge caution "just don't get it." Those who do "get it" can feel superior, believing that they are considerably above average in intelligence. Those less sure of themselves may join the herd because they think others know something that they themselves do not. This type of herding can sometimes even be rational in the presence of asymmetries in information.

As in the housing price bubble which led to the subprime crisis in the US, confirmation bias can lead to warning signs that conflict with the dominant narratives being heavily discounted. Indicators such as price–earnings ratios may be considered no longer relevant in the new situation, and the history of past bubbles and crashes overlooked. Fear of missing out can draw others in and keep the bubble going. With respect to real estate, another consideration can be the fear that if one doesn't buy now, they will soon be priced out of the market.

The developments described so far, while typically not fully rational, are not wildly irrational. However, at some point as the bubble continues, some investors may become carried away in a frenzy of greed and euphoria, an example of the wisdom of crowds turning into the madness of crowds.[48] Perhaps the most important factor influencing whether crowds display wisdom or madness is the extent to which individual decisions are made independently or not. It is when markets or crowds become dominated by the same idea or narrative, or euphoria, that they are most likely to display madness.[49]

Some participants in bubbles may have rational reasons although they likely suffer from hubris. The idea is to ride the bubble up, making profits along the way, but then pulling out shortly before it crashes.[50] They expect to profit from the irrationality of other participants. This strategy can be quite risky, however, since getting the timing right may be extremely difficult.[51] Overconfidence likely plays an important role for the fund managers who try this strategy.[52]

---

48 This last stage is not typical of all bubbles but is assumed in many discussions of historical bubbles. For recent analysis and history of discussions of the madness of crowds, see Bernstein (2021).

49 A related issue is the efficiency of group decision making. Reaching decisions in groups can be more efficient than those by a single decision maker where they bring in different perspectives. On the other hand, they can also lead to the perils of group think. See Perlmutter et al. (2024), chapter 15.

50 See, for example, the analysis and references in Brunnermeir and Reis (2023), chapter 2.

51 The literature has produced models of such behavior under the name of rational speculative bubbles. It is important to recognize, however, that only some of the participants in the bubble can be rational, or it would not start in the first place.

52 It is interesting that many fund managers, even when they are sure the market is in a bubble, will not choose to bet against it. This can be quite rational since many investors, especially at the retail level, may have short time horizons and do extrapolate the recent past into the future. Bubbles can sometimes last for a considerable period of time, and while they are continuing bear speculators will be earning below market returns. This in turn may cost them many clients and

Cognitive limitations, as distinct from psychological biases, certainly account for part of the tendency of decision makers to acquire insufficient knowledge about facts and the appropriate frameworks for analyzing them. Acquiring information can be costly, and it is often difficult to determine when the costs of obtaining more information begin to exceed the benefits.[53] Likely much more important than underinvesting in acquiring factual information, however, is the tendency to put too much faith in single conceptual frameworks or narratives to interpret the available facts.[54]

Extreme examples of hubris are typically outliers, but in milder forms they are not unusual. Furthermore, the conviction that one is right, combined with the desire to not be wrong, generates one of the most dangerous of behavioral biases, confirmation bias.[55] The combination of these traits is an important explanation for why crises often generate such strong responses. The new signals generated by a crisis can be so dramatic that they often override even strong cases of confirmation bias. The resulting realization that one's narrative was seriously defective would typically prompt much stronger reactions than that the crisis was just a bad draw from a known probability distribution.[56]

Recognition that one no longer understands the situation can understandably lead to extreme risk aversion, resulting in investors running for the exits. This helps explain why initial mild contagion from crises is often widespread, with later contagion becoming stronger and much more focused as investors begin to formulate new views.

In a complex world characterized by considerable uncertainty, the adoption of a view that turns out to be wrong is no sure sign of irrationality, and it can

hurt their own incomes as a result. Even with large private investors the adage may apply that the market can stay irrational longer than you can stay liquid.

53 There is also a bias toward focusing on the information that is most easily available. This is, of course, to some extent quite rational but may often be carried further than is optimal. For example, in the run-up to the Asian crisis, most of the macroeconomic information easily available on computer screens in New York or London were generally quite favorable, while information on misallocations of recent investments was less visible. An economist friend of mine became convinced that a crisis was lurking when he visited an Asian country and discovered that many of the recently built office buildings were half empty. Such observations played an important role in uncovering the substantial over-building which took place in China in the 2020s and led to the subsequent crisis in the real estate market.

54 One should also be concerned about the absence of potentially relevant information such as when Mexico stopped publishing their figures on international reserves, which turned out to be an important warning signal of their subsequent crisis.

55 Such hubris can be highly dangerous. I am reminded of an economist friend of mine who advised a young investment manager in a large New York bank well before the Mexican crisis of 1994 that a crisis appeared likely. The response he received was the comment, "why should I pay attention to you? Do you know how much money I made last year?"

56 Of course, not everyone will necessarily admit that they had been operating under a faulty perspective. For example, during the global financial crisis one high level bank official argued that they had been hit by a high sigma shock, one that would only happen every few billion years.

sometimes be difficult to judge whether a particular view was plausible ex ante or more the result of oversimplified or wishful thinking. What we can say, however, is that in a world of uncertainty it is not rational to base decisions only on a single perspective. Hubris and overconfidence are major contributors leading to beliefs in one's superiority in selecting the correct view and ignoring others.

Capital flows tend to generate much more complex effects and have a broader range of motivations than domestic asset purchases, and thus would seem likely to be less influenced by price dynamics that feed on themselves.[57] However, this is not to say that there are no such effects. As with bubbles, they seldom if ever begin from mood swings. Frequently there will be developments in the recipient countries which justify substantial capital inflows. New governments which undertook financial liberalization policies and adopted sound economic policies attracted large capital flows into East Asia, Mexico, and Argentina in the 1990s, while joining the euro area with the concomitant required policy reforms was the primary cause of the large capital inflows into several Southern European countries. The strong domestic economic conditions likewise induced domestic corporations and financial institutions to borrow more from abroad to obtain greater leverage.

On the push side, loose financial conditions in the advanced economies contribute to the size of such flows and may even be initiating forces, as low interest rates stimulate institutions to stretch for yield and increase investments in assets with higher expected returns and, of course, higher risks. This makes investing in emerging markets more attractive, while the easy financial conditions make more funds available to invest.

While less the result of price dynamics in asset markets, such capital flows are often increased by herding in popular narratives or mental models. This is particularly dangerous when markets tend to converge on a single paradigm. One of the reasons that such flows may become excessive is that, while it is relatively easy to see developments that make investments more attractive, it is generally more difficult to analyze when a country's capacity has been reached or when its stock has become overvalued.

Stock market booms do not always end in crashes. Likewise, many capital flow surges do not end in disruptive sudden stops and reversals.[58] When they do, it is seldom due primarily to investor mood swings. Often there are developments

[57] Some capital flows go directly into asset markets abroad and may be influenced by price dynamics in those markets as well as some of the behavioral biases just discussed.

[58] On the behavior of capital flow surges and reversals, see the analysis and references in Bird (2016), Efremidze et al. (2017), and Ghosh et al. (2019). On the similarities between stock market bubbles and capital flow surges, see Efremidze et al. (2016).

such as the elections of populist governments or unexpected crises in the recipient countries that lead to major reevaluations of views. While such events in themselves should lead to a decline in capital flows, often these reevaluations of views lead to much larger outflows than if the initial situation had been in equilibrium. While some of these reactions may well be due to investor and borrower panic, often these large outflows may be the result of recognition that a disequilibrium situation had developed where their financial positions are much riskier than originally thought, just as a small spark can set off a crash of an overvalued stock market.[59]

6.2 Limits to Arbitrage and International Capital Mobility

Limits to arbitrage are an important condition for making behavioral finance relevant. An essential assumption of efficient market theory is that, unlike in political voting where irrational votes are not offset by rational votes, in financial markets irrational market participants create profit opportunities. Taking advantage of these, rational speculation would offset the effects of the irrational participants, but as discussed earlier there are risks and costs to engaging in arbitrage, and not all rational investors may act on their assessments of the market. Another possibility would be if all participants became irrational, as could occur in the case of the madness of crowds leading to widespread panic.

For international monetary and financial analysis, an obvious implication is that, if behavioral biases are operative, then expectations in the foreign exchange market may display a wider range than just the static expectations assumed in the well-known Mundell–Fleming (MF) model or the rational expectations often assumed in more recent open-economy macro models. A review of the different capital flow assumptions of major types of open economy macro models will be discussed in the following section. A further implication is that international capital mobility will be less than perfect even if there are no formal restrictions on capital flows. This has major implications for a number of important issues, such as the effects of monetary and fiscal policies, and of sterilized intervention in the foreign exchange market.

One key implication that is often overlooked is that excessive exchange rate volatility may result not only from destabilizing speculation but also from a lack of stabilizing speculation. Because of lags in adjustments in real sectors, such as exports and imports, various types of shocks may create differences between short-term and longer-term equilibrium prices in the absence of speculation. In such circumstances, there are profit opportunities to take advantage of

[59] Not all of the shocks occur in the recipient countries. A fall in commodity prices or a tightening of monetary conditions in the advance economies are among the possible external causes.

expectations of how prices will adjust from the short-term to the long-run equilibrium, although uncertainty may greatly reduce the willingness of speculators to take advantage of these expected price and exchange rate movements. Such speculation would move the price or exchange rate adjustments forward to the longer-run equilibrium level and thus reduce price volatility.

For example, large sudden outflows of capital during the Asian crisis of 1997–98, caused in part by the wake-up call generated by the devaluation of the Thai baht, led to substantial exchange rate depreciation for a number of Asian economies. A considerable portion of these depreciations were afterwards reversed, leading to many charges that these over-depreciations were caused by panic and destabilizing speculation (Willett et al., 2004). However, this overshooting of the exchange rates is also consistent with an insufficiency of stabilizing speculation resulting in part from the huge amount of uncertainty that had been generated. Trade elasticities are often fairly low in the short run, so the longer-term adjustments of the trade balance to the capital flows would take some time.[60] In the absence of stabilizing speculation, the result is overshooting of exchange rate.

Analytically, the degree of capital mobility refers to the amount of capital that will flow in response to a unit change in incentives.[61] For different types of capital flows, the relevant incentives may differ. For example, for highly risk averse investors who wish to avoid the risk of exchange rate fluctuations, the relevant incentive is deviation from covered interest rate parity, that is, the interest rate differential adjusted for the cost of forward cover.

On the other hand, for risk-neutral international investors, the relevant incentives would be determined by deviations from uncovered interest rate parity (UIP), the interest differential adjusted for expectations of changes in the value of the currency over the life of the investment. If changes in interest rates are accompanied by changes in the exchange rate expectations, the incentives for capital flows may not change.[62]

While some empirical studies have investigated the determinants of international capital flows, they tend to focus on the comparative importance of different push and pull factors such as financial conditions in the advanced

---

[60] This is the famous J-curve effect where depreciation may initially worsen the trade balance in the short run because of low elasticities, but lead to improvements in the longer term. Without stabilizing speculation this would lead to overshooting of depreciation in the short term.

[61] For a review of the empirical literature on interest rate parity and the degree of international capital mobility, see the text by Pilbeam (2021) and the recent papers by Albagli et al. (2024) and Kalemi-Ocan and Varela (2024).

[62] The focus of this discussion is liquid debt instruments. The incentives for other types of investments such as direct investment and stock purchases would obviously differ, but these also would usually be influenced by the risk of exchange rate fluctuations, although direct investment would generally be less so.

economies and inflation and policy reforms in developing countries, rather than the degree of capital mobility per se.[63] Much more testing has focused on the efficiency of the foreign exchange market by looking at whether profit opportunities generated by interest differentials are arbitraged or speculated away.

These studies generally find that between countries with well-developed financial markets and no capital controls, covered interest parity (CIP) generally holds. In general, capital flows coupled with the purchase of forward contracts work to eliminate the risk of exchange rate changes.[64] This is especially true of the euro currency markets. However, contrary to what is sometimes argued, this does not necessarily mean that capital mobility is perfect. Deviations from covered interest rate parity offer clear evidence that capital mobility is imperfect, but the converse does not hold. If there is a great deal of uncertainty and market participants are hesitant to take on uncovered positions, then a fairly small capital flow may be sufficient to close the covered differential, but it would take much larger capital flows for UIP to hold. Thus, CIP is not an appropriate measure of the degree of capital mobility.[65]

Tests of uncovered interest differentials give a much better test of exchange market efficiency than those of covered arbitrage. With UIP, any interest rate differentials would be matched by expected equivalent changes in exchange rates. What would be gained by investing in higher interest rate assets abroad would be offset by losses because of depreciation of the exchange rate. While we often do not have good measures of exchange rate expectations, this condition can be tested by whether the interest rate differential is an unbiased predictor of the future spot rate.

There have been many tests of UIP across a wide range of countries and time periods. While some of these studies find that UIP holds for particular currencies and time periods, most do not.[66] As Albagli et al. (2024) write: "While the uncovered interest rate parity (UIP) has long been at the core of international macroeconomics, few relationships have received a starker rejection in empirical work" (p. 1). This indicates that the simple efficient market hypothesis often does not hold in this context. However, the simple version assumes risk neutrality. The more general theory of efficient markets drops this assumption

63 See, for example, the review by Hannan (2018).

64 See, for example, the analysis and references in Kalemi-Ocan and Varela (2024). On the issue of home country bias, see Greenspan (2014) and Obstfeld and Rogoff (2000).

65 For a detailed explanation see Willett et al. (2002). Unfortunately, the size of deviations from UIP do not provide information about how much capital will flow in response to a change in incentives.

66 This failure of UIP to hold is often called the forward premium puzzle. This is because while CIP does not imply UIP, UIP does imply CIP, so in an efficient market the forward premia and the interest differential would be equal.

and allows for efficient risk premia. In this case, higher expected returns are due only to higher risks.

There were conflicting interpretations of the findings that simple UIP often did not hold. One school took this as an indication that the market was not efficient, and others that it must mean that there is a time-varying risk premium. It is not easy to clearly distinguish between these two interpretations, but the failure to find that various proxies for risk explain a considerable part of the deviations suggests that many foreign exchange markets, including some for the advanced economies, are not fully efficient. In the absence of capital controls this could be due to nonrational expectations or limited capital mobility, that is, limits to arbitrage, or both.

While tests of UIP focus particularly on flows of liquid shorter-term instruments, there is also evidence of limited capital mobility for other types of capital flows, such as the home bias in portfolio investments. For portfolio investments, many studies have demonstrated substantial home bias. Likewise, international correlations between domestic output and consumption conflict with the theory that full advantage is being taken of the opportunities for international capital flows to improve the intertemporal optimization of consumption.

We still do not fully understand all of the reasons why arbitrage is limited, even in domestic financial markets. The fact that arbitrage can be highly risky at times is certainly one of the most important reasons. Prohibitions on short selling also often limit the extent of speculation against bubbles. Furthermore, access to assets and borrowing power of those willing to bet against the market is likely to be limited.

When it comes to international capital flows, the possible reasons for limitations become even stronger. To many economists, government regulations like capital controls first come to mind as the reason why all international profit opportunities are not exploited, but there are a number of other reasons as well. Desired information about international investments is often limited and costly to obtain. While basic macroeconomic data for most countries is now fairly easily available, these may sometimes give a seriously misleading picture of the true situation. This was true in the run-up to the Asian crisis. The perception that foreign investment is inherently riskier than domestic investments is still widespread and likely has a substantial impact on retail investors. Many still do not understand the full benefits of diversification. This, of course, does not apply to the fund managers, but it does limit the amount of retail funds they have to manage.

In summary, there is considerable evidence that capital mobility, while often quite high, is frequently less than perfect. Markets often behave with neither static nor rational expectations, as is assumed in most popular international monetary and macro models. This has important implications for international monetary and financial analysis, which will be explored in the following section.

7 The Nature of the Capital Flow Assumptions in the Major Open Economy Macro Models

The most popular open economy macroeconomic models often make quite different assumptions about the behavior of international capital flows and financial markets.[67] These can differ both about the extent of capital mobility and about how expectations are formed. Many of the newer models assume perfect capital mobility and rational expectations. These models give us important insights, but they cannot be relied upon to offer full explanations for the behavior of international capital flows and their implications for foreign exchange markets and macroeconomic policies, nor can they provide a foolproof guide for international investors. Some of the older models, such as MF, despite their serious deficiencies for some purposes, remain highly useful for others. Analysts and policymakers need to be aware of the full range of such models and attempt to develop a sense of which models are most useful under which circumstances.

This section explains the key assumptions of the major models with respect to international capital mobility and the behavior of foreign exchange and international financial markets, and discusses their major strengths and weaknesses. Particular attention is given to the extent to which they are consistent with efficient market theory and the behavioral finance approach outlined in the study.

7.1 Mundell–Fleming Models

Probably the most well-known international macro model is the traditional MF model. While it is used a good bit less today in advanced economic research, and there are updated versions that make alternative assumptions about wage and price stickiness and expectations, the traditional model is still the workhorse of most international and macroeconomics texts.

The traditional version is based on a simple short-run fixed price Keynesian macro model that is extended to take into account trade balances, exchange rates, and international capital flows. It is particularly famous for its analysis of how the degree of capital mobility and fixed versus flexible exchange rates

[67] Here we tend to focus on the strongest forms of these models. More details on the models and their evolution are given in any mainstream modern macroeconomics text. In many of these texts, emphasis may differ considerably from the perspectives offered here.

affect the strength of domestic monetary and fiscal policies. For example, monetary policy is strongest under flexible exchange rates and loses all of its potency under fixed rates with perfect capital mobility. Under fixed rates, fiscal expansions can generate either balance of payments surpluses or deficits, depending on whether the effects on capital flows are greater or less than the effects on the current account. Likewise, under flexible rates, fiscal expansion can lead to either appreciation or depreciation.[68]

Other important contributions include its focus on the importance of how fiscal deficits are financed, its analysis of the international transmission of various shocks, and the delineation of optimal monetary, fiscal, and exchange rate polices in response to them. It is important, however, to keep in mind that the MF model focuses only on short-term demand effects and assumes that governments are creditworthy. This short-run focus means that the model does not deal well with economic growth and with the medium as well as longer-term effects of monetary and fiscal policies as wages and prices become more flexible over time.[69] Its neglect of the role of expectations limits its appropriate applications to cases of unanticipated policy changes which are expected to be permanent. In other words, it assumes static expectations. Another crucial limitation is that the model assumes a flow theory of capital flows, which is inconsistent with modern finance theory. As a result, its usefulness is limited to the short run. This will be discussed in the following section on the international monetary trilemma.

The model also has important implications for the degree to which international financial markets provide discipline over domestic macroeconomic policies. In the model, under fixed exchange rates, high capital mobility provides strong discipline over domestic monetary policy. However, contrary to the popular view that financial markets provide healthy discipline over domestic macroeconomic policies in general, it indicates that under fixed rates international capital mobility makes it easier to finance fiscal deficits, since the capital inflows limit the degree to which interest rates rise in response to larger fiscal deficits. This case of anti-discipline fits well the case of Argentina's currency board, where capital flows provided strong discipline over monetary

[68] Explanations for these conclusions can be found in almost any text on international macro or monetary economics. Despite their short-term nature, the MF models tend to assume longer-run trade elasticities, so they do not consider the effect of depreciation leading to an initial worsening of the trade balance due to low trade elasticities in the short run.

[69] Early on many users did not recognize that its useful applicability was limited to the short run. Over time, many of the qualifications initially raised by monetary critics were incorporated into mainstream macro models, an important example of positive evidence eventually winning out over initial intellectual commitments to particular models. However, confirmation bias on both sides slowed this process a good deal.

policy but helped finance the continued financing of large fiscal deficits. The Greek fiscal crisis provides another example.

Besides static expectations, the types of herding discussed in the section on capital flow surges can also help explain cases where international financial markets do not provide discipline. For financial market discipline to work, expectations must be forward looking, reasonably rational, and based on reasonable information. The MF model assumes that the solvency of countries is not at issue, while concerns over future solvency are often a primary factor in the cases where financial markets do provide discipline by providing early warning signals of emerging problems. These different possibilities offer important examples of how different mechanisms of expectations formation can have extremely important implications and why markets may behave differently at different times.[70]

Another difficulty with the MF and many other international macro models is that they focus only on net capital flows. For some purposes this is quite important, but for a number of international financial issues a focus on gross capital flows is essential.[71] For example, the study of capital flow surges and reversals has shown that there are often important differences in the behavior of gross and net capital flows. Likewise, a major part of the spread of the US subprime crisis to Europe was through the interdependence of two-way gross flows that would not show up in an analysis focusing only on net flows. European banks had invested heavily in US subprime securities but had financed them largely by borrowing from US money market funds. Thus, despite having little net exposure to US financial institutions, they were highly exposed to the US financial crisis.

Despite the many criticisms that the model has drawn, it has proven to be quite useful in explaining many short run developments. However, neglect of expectations limits its appropriate applications, as it assumes static expectations.[72] As emphasized in later literature, in many cases this assumption is seriously misleading.[73] However, often

policy changes are largely unanticipated, and agents may have diverse expectations, so that policy changes that are anticipated by some may still be unanticipated by others.

[70] For further discussion, see the analysis and references in Willett, Chiu, and Walter (2014).

[71] See Borio et al. (2017) and Obstfeld and Taylor (2017).

[72] There have been many additions incorporated into versions of the MF model that help deal with some of these issues.

[73] For example, they fostered early beliefs that the Phillips curve showed that there was a long-run trade-off between higher unemployment and inflation, while the important contributions by Friedman and Phelps showed that over time expectations would adjust, and the longer-term trade-off would disappear. See any major textbook on macroeconomics.

Expectations formation is also extremely important for the extent to which international financial markets provide discipline with respect to monetary and fiscal policies. With static expectations, as assumed in the MF model, high capital mobility would help governments finance deficits with lower interest rates and hence help them continue to run excessive deficits. This is not just a theoretical curiosity but has occurred on many occasions, such as the Greek fiscal crisis.[74] It would require fairly good information and forward-looking expectations for markets to recognize these problems and begin to demand higher risk premia which in turn would serve as early warning signals. Markets have been quite variable in the extent to which they have provided such signals.

The real effects of monetary and fiscal policies will be determined not only by the degree of capital mobility and exchange rate regime, as in the original MF model, but also by the extent to which economic agents are forward looking, the degree to which policy actions are anticipated, and the extent of wage and price flexibility. As stressed in the early new classical macro models, with flexible wages and prices, monetary policies will only have real effects if they are unanticipated.[75] However, there is often a good deal of wage price stickiness in the short run. Furthermore, while empirical research shows that there are some regularities in policy reaction functions, their unexplained variance is often quite considerable.[76]

7.2. The International Monetary Trilemma

One of the most frequently used concepts in international monetary analysis is the international monetary trilemma.[77] It states that countries cannot have at the same time fixed exchange rates, independent monetary policies, and the absence

---

[74] For further discussion of this issue. see Willett et al. (2014).

[75] See any standard macroeconomics text.

[76] Furthermore, even anticipated policy changes may have real effects if the extent of the change is not fully anticipated. For example, it was widely expected that the Federal Reserve would begin to lower interest rates in the fall of 2024 but there was considerable uncertainty over whether the initial cut would be 25 or 50 basis points.

[77] For further analysis, see the discussion and references in Willett and Bird (2024). This trilemma does not say that countries must go all the way to the extremes of floating exchange rates to obtain a degree of monetary dependence. It rather implies that the greater is the degree of exchange rate flexibility, the greater will be the degree of feasible monetary policy independence. In fact, few countries go all the way to the extremes of free floating or absolutely fixed rates. This is explained by the theory of optimal currency areas, which indicates that relatively few countries meet the conditions for freely floating or permanently fixed exchange rates. While many criteria have been developed, one of the most important is the size and openness of economies, with fixed rates working best for very small open economies such as Panama, and floating rates for very large economies such as the US. See the analysis and references in Dellas and Tavlas (2009) and Willett (2003).

of capital controls.[78] The trilemma is often justified in terms of the MF model, which shows that with perfect capital mobility and fixed exchange rates, monetary policy is ineffective. Any domestic efforts at undertaking independent monetary policy actions would be fully offset by international capital flows. It has not always been sufficiently recognized, however, that as is discussed in the section on capital mobility, capital controls are not the only reason why capital mobility may be limited. In such cases sterilization of capital flows can allow countries to operate outside of the trilemma constraints in the short run. Thus, the international monetary dilemma provides long-run constraints on countries' policy options but provides short-run constraints only in the case of very high capital mobility.

The trilemma is an application of the theory of economic policy, which demonstrates that, in general, to achieve a given number of policy objectives one must have at least that number of independent policy instruments. In the international monetary context, it was generally assumed that countries have two major policy objectives: internal and external balance.[79] External balance was defined as the need for balance of payments equilibrium over the medium or long term, while internal balance was defined as the best feasible combination of inflation and unemployment. Three main policy instruments could be used to achieve needed balance of payments adjustments: exchange rate changes, capital controls, and changes in monetary policy. With fixed exchange rates ruling out the use of exchange rate changes, and a prohibition on controls, domestic monetary policy would be the only remaining policy instrument. However, using monetary policy to restore external balance would often conflict with its use to achieve internal balance. For example, if a country had high inflation but a balance of payments surplus, tightening monetary policy to reduce inflation would also increase the balance of payments surplus.

The Bretton Woods system was based on having exchange rates fixed in the short run but adjustable in situations such as just described, where there was a conflict between the uses of domestic policy to achieve internal and external equilibrium. The IMF called such situations ones of fundamental disequilibrium, and recommended exchange rate adjustments.[80] In the case of payments

[78] There is also an international financial trilemma which argues that you cannot have all three of no capital controls, independent financial regulation and the absence of financial crises. This trilemma points more to the need for the international coordination of financial policies rather than providing a set of binding constraints as does the international monetary trilemma. There is also likely to be less divergence across countries in optimal financial regulations than in monetary policies. See Willett and Bird (2024).

[79] Of course they will have many other less important objectives as well.

[80] As countries became increasingly reluctant to change exchange rates as the Bretton Woods international monetary system evolved, many began to refer to it as an international disequilibrium system.

imbalances that were not likely to be persistent, the Bretton Woods philosophy was to keep the exchange rate fixed and use international reserves to finance the payments imbalances. As the MF model shows, such delaying of adjustments would be feasible under fixed rates only if capital mobility was less than perfect. However, in the early days of Bretton Woods, there were still extensive exchange controls that had been put on during WWII, so the assumption of imperfect capital mobility was quite reasonable.

With imperfect capital mobility, the effects of international capital flows on the domestic money supply can be offset by domestic open market operations to sterilize the effects of the capital flows on the domestic money supply, thus giving short-term monetary independence. Such sterilization provides an additional policy instrument. This works, however, only in the short run since it allows payment imbalances to continue and they cannot continue to do so forever.[81] The ability to sterilize capital flows in the short run has the benefit of giving countries an extra degree of freedom to operate outside of the trilemma constraints in the short run. If used well, this can be welfare enhancing. However, it also creates the problem, discussed in the section on currency crises, that countries may delay needed adjustments for too long, resulting in currency crises. As we will discuss, behavioral biases tend to worsen this problem.

As the Bretton Woods era progressed, beliefs that capital flows were inherently unstable declined, and the reduction in capital controls combined with improvements in technology, led to much larger capital flows. As a result, the size of capital flows during crises increased substantially and the extent to which countries could successfully postpone adjustments decreased. The resulting frequency of major currency crises increased, and these were a major contributor to the breakdown of the Bretton Woods system of adjustably pegged exchange rates.[82]

The frequency with which adjustable peg exchange rate regimes became associated with currency crises gave rise to the popularity of the bipolar or unstable middle hypothesis that, in conditions of high capital mobility, countries needed to move away from adjustable peg regimes, which offered what was called a one-way speculative option.[83] Private agents didn't know whether an exchange rate would be adjusted at any particular moment, but they could be

[81] At least if one does not have a currency that is used for international reserves such as the dollar. Even with the dollar, its longer deficits became a serious problem and contributed importantly to the breakdown of the Bretton Woods system. See the analysis and references in Willett (1977).

[82] Again, see the analysis and references in Willett (1977).

[83] The strong bipolar hypothesis said that countries needed to move all the way to one of the extremes of permanently fixed or floating rates, while the more moderate unstable middle hypothesis suggested that countries could reduce substantially the incidence of currency crises

sure of the direction in which it would be moved if it were changed. A deficit country would only devalue its currency, while a surplus country would only revalue it. The higher the international capital mobility, the quicker crises would occur if currencies remained overvalued. The tendency to delay adjustments too long can be explained in substantial part by the combination of time inconsistency problems, wishful thinking, and political economy considerations, and are likely to be more important in situations of considerable uncertainty.[84]

The validity of the trilemma analysis has been challenged from several directions. In the 1960s, Mundell argued that fiscal policy could offer an additional policy tool. For example, with tighter monetary policy and easier fiscal policy, the resulting increase in interest rates would attract greater capital inflows to reduce a payments deficit, while the expansionary fiscal policy would offset the contractionary effects of tight money and keep the economy at full employment. With the flow theory of capital flows contained in the MF model, these increased capital inflows would continue indefinitely. However, this would be inconsistent with the portfolio balance considerations emphasized in modern finance theory. Investors would adjust their portfolios to reflect the change in the interest differential, but once they had done this, investors would not have incentives to continue adjustments and generate continuous capital flows.

To generate persistent large capital inflows, continuously increasing interest rates would be required. A given level of monetary tightening would only improve the balance of payments in the short run. Thus, adjustments in the monetary fiscal mix should be viewed as a way of financing a deficit, similar to running down reserves, rather than as a method of balance of payments adjustment. In other words, from the standpoint of the theory of economic policy, monetary and fiscal policy would be independent instruments only in the short run, just as in the case of using international reserves to finance payments imbalances.[85]

From the other direction, Rey (2013) has argued that because exchange adjustments are ineffective, there is only a dilemma, with independent monetary policy requiring capital controls. While gaining a good deal of attention, her argument that exchange rate flexibility generally is not effective in giving greater monetary independence has not been widely accepted, although it is

by moving away from adjustable peg regimes without having to move all the way to one of the extremes. Angkinand et al. (2009) offer empirical support for the latter version.

84 While a full analysis goes beyond the scope of this Element, see the analysis and references in Bird and Willett (2008), Walter and Willett (2012), Willett, Chiu, and Walter (2014), and Amri and Willett (2017).

85 See Willett and Forte (1969).

likely true for very small open economies, as shown in the theory of optimal currency areas. See, for example, the analysis and references in Willett (2003).

A key issue is the meaning of the effectiveness of exchange rate flexibility for the independence of monetary policy. It is well known that flexible rates cannot insulate countries completely from foreign shocks. Thus, no economy can be fully independent of what is going on in the world economy. However, exchange rate adjustments can give countries the ability to use monetary policy to respond to both domestic and international shocks in a way that is not possible under fixed exchange rates.

7.3 Monetary Models

The earliest Keynesian models were seriously deficient in terms of giving attention to monetary policy. This was partially corrected in the MF model since it explicitly included monetary policy. From the perspective of monetarists, however, monetary policy in the MF model was still formulated in a deficient way.

The simple monetary models provide a very different perspective from the Keynesian-based MF model.[86] They assume a good deal of wage and price flexibility, and, as a result, purchasing parity holds over the long run. Some models assume it also holds in the short run. While the MF models assume that interest rate increases will be associated with currency appreciation, the monetary models imply just the opposite. Currencies with higher interest rates will have depreciating currencies.

Which model predicts correctly? In truth, both are part right and part wrong. Sometimes the relationship goes one way and sometimes the other. However, this does not reflect a fundamental difference in the economic theory involved. The models vary both in the structures of the economy that underlie them and the nature of the important shocks that are assumed to face them. The MF model assumes that an increase in nominal interest rates is due to an increase in real interest rates, for example, due to an unanticipated tightening of monetary policy and will be associated with currency appreciation.

The monetary models usually make the Fisher (1930) assumption that the real interest rate is constant, so that any increase in the nominal interest rate is due to an increase in inflationary expectations. In this case, we would expect the currency to depreciate. The Fisher open version assumes that the real exchange

[86] See, for example, Milton Friedman's (1953) classic article in favor of flexible exchange rates. On the evolution of arguments for flexible rates, see Tavlas (2024). Keynesians were split on fixed versus flexible exchange rates. A small group of monetarists led by Art Laffer and Robert Mundell later began to argue for fixed rates. Discussion of this issue goes beyond the scope of the Element.

rate is constant as well as the real interest rate. Therefore, purchasing power parity (PPP) also holds, as does UIP.[87] In all the monetary models, this relationship holds in the long run, but in some they may not hold in the short run, especially for unanticipated changes in monetary policy.[88]

The evidence indicates that in the short run interest rates change in response both to changes in inflationary expectations and to factors affecting real interest rates. Furthermore, because expectations are often hard to pinpoint, at times the causes of changes in interest rates may be subject to considerable uncertainty, giving rise to differing narratives. This offers another illustration that we should not expect any one model to be appropriate for all situations.[89]

7.4 Intertemporal Optimization Models of the New Classical Macroeconomics

Much of the effort in both domestic and open economy macroeconomic models in recent decades has gone into developing theories based on explicit microeconomics-based optimizing analysis of rational agents.[90] While older macroeconomic models tended to be based on assumptions which were often plausible from a microeconomic perspective, such as if income goes up people will consume more and if interest rates go up investment will fall, these were generally not based on analysis of fully optimizing behavior. Thus, these newer efforts make important contributions. However, they face the difficulty that to be manageable mathematically, they can focus on only a limited set of considerations. This is true of all models, but there has been an unfortunate tendency by some users of these models to treat considerations outside of the

[87] Perfect capital mobility and infinite trade elasticities, such as tend to hold in small open economies, which are price takers, are sufficient conditions for PPP and UIP to hold. They are not necessary conditions, however. These relationships could hold even for countries with little economic and financial interdependence because of the nature of monetary models. This helps explain why, unlike the MF models, many of the monetary models do not focus on the degree of capital mobility. Neither type of model considers the possibility of destabilizing speculation.

[88] The well-known paper by Dornbusch (1976) combines elements of monetary models and the sticky price assumptions of Keynesian models with the assumptions of perfect capital mobility to investigate the effects of unanticipated monetary expansion on the behavior of floating exchange rates. Like many of the monetary models, it assumes that purchasing power parity, or PPP, holds in the long run but not in the short run. In this model the monetary expansion leads initially to over-depreciation, with the currency then rising toward the new PPP level. While intellectually attractive, this model has only limited explanatory power.

[89] It also illustrates the important general principle that the correlations among the two dependent variables, such as asset prices, interest rates, and exchange rates, will vary depending on the shocks they face.

[90] The classic reference is Lucas and Sargent (1978). This approach was appropriately labeled new classical because it tended to assume high flexible wages and prices even in the short run, and drew many of the same conclusions about macroeconomic policy as did the original classical economists. The application of this approach to international macroeconomics was strongly influenced by Obstfeld and Rogoff's (1996) masterful book.

model as being irrelevant. This reminds one of the comment that it is usually better to be roughly right than precisely wrong.

Of course, a main feature of behavioral economics is that people's behavior is not always rational and they often face considerable uncertainty. While macroeconomics has paid a good deal of attention to factors such as imperfect information and uncertainty, so far there has been much less explicit introduction of behavioral factors into macroeconomic and exchange rate models than into financial economics.[91] Still, it can be useful to take into consideration the less rigorous but often pertinent insights from earlier macro models and behavioral considerations. They provide powerful critiques of some of the conclusions drawn by a number of the new classical macroeconomics.

Much of the new classical literature focused on intertemporal optimization of consumption streams. Early Keynesian analysis made the simple assumption that consumption depends on the level of current income. As a starting point, this seems to be quite a reasonable but incomplete first step for short-run analysis. Unfortunately, some of the prominent early Keynesian economists overlooked this limitation and assumed that this simple assumption would work for the long term as well. This led to the very pessimistic conclusion that since the marginal propensity to consume was less than one, over time consumption would not keep up with the growth in income, and an increasing glut of savings would occur.

This potential problem, which was called the secular stagnation hypothesis, had similar predictions to standard Marxist analysis that workers would be kept at subsistence levels so that there would be increasing savings gluts, resulting in cumulative capitalist crises. Alvin Hansen (1953) of Harvard (1953) was the most prominent advocate of this secular stagnation view. While he put forward a number of arguments for this conclusion, the implications of the standard Keynesian consumption function were the most influential.[92] Keynesian economics provided a solution to this problem. Increasing savings gluts could be offset by expansionary fiscal policies. Fortunately, most workers' incomes did not remain at subsistence levels, nor did the ratios of consumption to income tend to increase over time. Indeed, the problem for many countries became too little rather than too much savings.

Modern macroeconomics highlights the crucial importance of factors other than current income that influence consumption, such as wealth or permanent income that shift up the Keynesian consumption functions as income grows

[91] Exceptions include De Grauwe and Grimaldi (2006) and De Grauwe and Ji (2019).

[92] For an analysis of the evolution of views on the secular stagnation hypothesis, see Backhouse and Boiannovsky (2016). More recently this concept has been revived by Summers (2013) with the addition of more sophisticated arguments. See also Acemoglu and Restrepo (2017).

over the longer term. The classic reference is Friedman (1957), which developed the permanent income hypothesis. Since then a number of other expansions of the simple Keynesian consumption function have been developed. (See any major macroeconomics text.) Modern macroeconomics also emphasizes the important distinctions between anticipated and unanticipated shocks, the degree of credibility of government debt, and permanent versus temporary changes in tax policies. Thus, for example, measures that offer temporary income tax cuts are likely to have considerably smaller effects on spending than permanent tax cuts. An example of this is President Johnson's temporary tax cut during the Vietnam War, which had very limited effects.

An extreme version of such analysis became popular among new classical economists. In this view, changes in taxes have no effect on aggregate demand. One could think of this Ricardian equivalence as an extreme version of such an analysis, where all changes in taxes are considered to be temporary.[93] The evidence does not generally support this extreme view.

Uncertainty and behavioral considerations help explain this result. Few, if any, individuals are sufficiently farsighted to weigh heavily events that may not take place for many decades, nor can individuals be certain of the structure of taxes they will face in the future. Thus, while the distinction between temporary and permanent tax cuts is important, its relevance is likely to be largely limited to cases where the reversal is expected to occur not too far in the future and where there is less uncertainty about the incidence of future taxes.

7.5 Capital Flows and Currency Crisis Models

While economists have analyzed the causes of currency crises for centuries, in the 1990s a formal literature devoted to currency attacks was developed and proved to be extremely influential among economists and researchers in international monetary and political economy.[94] These models have generally been categorized as falling into three generations. The first-generation models focused on cases of fundamental disequilibrium in which crises were inevitable and only the timing was in question.

[93] In this model, all tax changes are treated as temporary on the assumption that they must be offset by opposite changes in taxes in the future. As a result, private savings change by an equal amount so as to optimize the stream of individuals' lifetime consumption. As a result of this offsetting shift in savings, consumption, investment, and the balance of payments are not affected by the changes in taxes. Ricardo himself viewed his analysis as an interesting exercise but not as a basis for prediction.

[94] See, for example, the discussion and references in the Pilbeam (2023) text. For convenience throughout, I refer to all such pressures in the foreign exchange market based on expectations of exchange rate changes as due to speculation, but they often include considerable amounts of funds moved by risk averse institutions and individuals seeking to avoid losses.

Second-generation models expanded the range of the fundamentals from just good or bad to include an intermediate category of fundamentals that were neither so strong that a crisis was unthinkable, nor so bad that one was inevitable. With fundamentals in this intermediate category, a country entered a vulnerable zone with multiple equilibria where crises were possible but not inevitable.

While these first two generations focused on flow disequilibria, the third generation drew on the literature of banking crises, focusing on the financial sector problems of inadequate liquidity and the potential for runs on currencies where liquid liabilities were high relative to countries' and financial institutions' reserves.[95] These considerations help to explain crises that hit countries that did not have initial balance of payments difficulties.

In a number of cases where there was confidence in financial sectors, large capital inflows financed current account deficits, such as in Indonesia and Korea in the mid 1990s. However, when wake-up calls led to the discovery of serious problems in the financial sectors, the capital inflows turned into outflows, and currencies which had not been overvalued quickly became so, leading to still further capital outflows.

The initial first-generation model was presented by Paul Krugman (1979). While highly influential in the academic community because of its attractive theoretical formulation, it was of little practical value. Because it assumed a small open economy with perfect capital mobility, the only warning signs of the looming crisis in the model were large, persistent fiscal deficits and losses of international reserves. The higher interest and inflation rates and monetary expansion that usually also accompany cases of fundamental disequilibrium are absent, and when the peg is forced to be abandoned there is no sharp depreciation, only the beginning of a gradual decline.[96]

The second-generation models are considerably more attractive in two respects. First, they consider cases where fundamentals are neither so bad that a crisis is inevitable nor so strong that a crisis is highly improbable. Many countries frequently fall into such zones of vulnerability where, even with fully rational speculation crises are possible but not inevitable. This gives rise to the possibilities of multiple equilibria and self-fulfilling speculation.

The second major improvement is that political economy considerations are introduced. Unlike the first-generation models, it is assumed that governments

[95] See, for example, Allen et al. (2009) and the discussion in Pilbeam (2013). An example is Morris and Shin (1998).

[96] These conclusions are the result of the assumption that the currency was initially substantially undervalued. The first-generation models are basically ones of fundamental disequilibrium, and this can be generated by a number of different factors.

have the power, but not necessarily the willingness, to undertake domestic adjustments to protect the currency. Thus, perceptions of likely government reactions to possible capital outflows become an important aspect of fundamentals.

While yielding important insights, tractability in modeling required the initial versions of these, and the third-generation models as well, to assume homogenous speculators and high capital mobility. These assumptions imply that crises would occur quickly and that speculative attacks will succeed. In practice, because of uncertainty, differences in expectations, and imperfect capital mobilities, crises often, although not always, extend over a considerable period of time and often do not succeed.[97]

Note that self-fulfilling speculation need not be irrational or unjustified, as Krugman (1996) wrongly argued. Some have gone so far as to incorrectly say that these models showed that even countries with strong fundamentals could face speculative attacks. This might occur, but not within the context of standard second-generation models. The formal crisis models generally assume rational expectations. Many of the claims of destabilizing speculation come from officials practicing blame avoidance. Such claims are also often made by private sector agents to explain why they did not see crises coming, another example of the trait of blame avoidance.

In such models, as countries enter a vulnerable zone, the markets would force up their interest rates to reflect the possibility of crises. In many cases, however, such increases did not occur, challenging the assumption of rational expectations. In these models, countries in the vulnerable zone who were attacked would be unlucky, but not innocent victims. This term should apply only to attacks based on destabilizing speculation or foreign shocks.

A second aspect of these models is that they do not specify what causes shifts in expectations. This is quite understandable from the standpoint of the feasibility of modeling, but what is unfortunate is that while causes of the shifts in expectations are outside of the model, the literal implication is that the shifts in expectations which generate the speculative attacks are purely arbitrary. While this is certainly a possibility, it is seldom the case. In the many crises that I have studied, the spark that sets off the crisis is usually a shock that generates wake-up calls, not arbitrary shifts in the expectations of private sector actors.[98]

97 Almamood et al. (2018).

98 For example, the spark that set off the crises in many East Asian countries in 1997 was the largely surprise devaluation of the Thai baht. This in turn was caused by the governments' discovery that the country had basically run out of international reserves in the central bank's attempts to defend the baht's peg, see Willett et al. (2004). This shock led to widespread recognition that financial positions in a number of countries were much more exposed to currency risk than had been thought.

It should be stressed that in particular crises, more than one of these types of models may give useful insights. For example, large fiscal deficits associated with reunification in Germany, combined with tight monetary policies, led to large capital flows from the other European economies into Germany. These policies generated a first-generation type situation of fundamental disequilibrium in the European monetary system in the 1990s as long as macroeconomic policies remained largely unchanged.[99] However, it was not clear for a good while whether this assumption of no major changes in the policies of the capital exporting and importing counties would be correct. There were substantial negotiations attempting to get Germany to take actions to lower its interest rates, and it did so to a small degree, but not nearly enough to reduce the major disequilibrium. As stressed in the second-generation models, policy reactions were crucial. If Germany had agreed to cut interest rates further, in exchange for substantial tightening in the other countries, the breakdown of the pegged rate system might have been avoided. This is an example of how political economy expectations could have an important effect, as is highlighted in the second-generation models.[100]

Another example of the applicability of multiple crisis models was the Asian Crisis. The Thai devaluation which set off the crisis was of the first-generation type, an overvalued currency. Countries like Korea did not obviously have this problem. However, many of the East Asian economies were in vulnerable zones because of problems in their financial sectors. As long as these problems were not widely recognized, it was reasonable to consider their fundamentals to be strong, although it was likely not reasonable to not have investigated their financial sectors more closely despite their lack of transparency. However, the Thai devaluations generated a wake-up call that led to the discovery of many second- and third-generation-type problems, especially in the financial sectors of a number of countries, including Thailand itself.[101]

---

[99] Incidentally, this episode presents a case of an innocent victim. France had stronger macroeconomic fundamentals than Germany, but the shock associated with German reunification changed France's roughly equilibrium exchange rate to an overvalued one. France was in a recession at the time, which made it unwilling to adopt the degree of tight domestic policies that would have been needed to successfully defend its currency peg.

[100] This case also illustrates the importance of the MF analysis. Because Germany's fiscal expansion was accompanied by tight monetary policy, high capital mobility led to a substantial balance of payments surplus. The large fiscal expansion in the US associated with the Vietnam War was accompanied by accommodative monetary policy. This led to large capital outflows and a US payments deficit which was the immediate cause of the breakdown of the Bretton Woods system.

[101] For further analysis, see Rajan (2001) and Willett et al. (2004) and the references cited there.

7.6 Contagion

The term "contagion" has been frequently used in different ways. The basic idea is clear. Contagion occurs when developments in one market, such as currency or financial crises or sharp drops in asset prices, lead to similar developments in other markets and often other countries.[102] However, contagion may have a number of different causes, transmission mechanisms, and types of effects.

Failure to specify what type of contagion one has in mind has often led to confusion, with evidence of contagion frequently taken as evidence of irrational behavior of the types emphasized in behavioral finance. Thus, for example, the contagion that occurred during the Asia crisis in 1997–98 has often been described as being due to irrational panic, but much of the panic was justified by conditions that had not been previously recognized, such as the severe problems in domestic financial sectors, combined with high levels of debt denominated in foreign currency, and the shattering of the idea that there could be no major depreciations, triggered by the huge depreciation of the Thai baht.[103] This was a classic case of a crisis generating a wake-up call for the private sector to reevaluate their financial positions.

Contagions can also vary considerably in terms of strength, and the failure to distinguish these varying strengths sometimes exaggerates the extent of damage that contagion does to the world economy. For example, the Asia crisis is sometimes discussed as having been felt across the globe. This was true, but the effects on most countries were very mild and of little consequence for policy. On the other hand, a number of East Asian countries were hit with major speculative attacks and capital flight, which had devastating consequences. Between these extremes are episodes which have substantial effects on foreign exchange markets and asset prices but which fall short of major crises. An example is the Russian crisis of 1998 where relatively few countries suffered major speculative attacks, but a number of emerging market countries lost their access to borrow from the global financial markets for a considerable period of time.

A full analysis of a particular episode of contagion needs to specify the events which stimulated the contagion, the types of causes of the contagion, the channels through which it operated, its strength and the factors which

[102] While contagion is usually thought of in terms of behavior during crisis, a form of contagion can also occur during boom periods and capital flow surges. Such contagion or herding often is not merely due to follow-the-leader behavior but can be importantly influenced by the spread of particular mental models or stories which motivate behavior. For discussion of such contagion in narratives, see Shiller (2020).

[103] In everyday usage the concept of rational panic may seem a contradiction, but in the economics literature a banking crisis is often called a banking panic and these may be quite rational at times when it is discovered that a bank's financial position is much worse than had been thought.

influenced its strength. These can vary greatly across episodes. Also important are the policies adopted to try to reduce its effects. For example, there is considerable evidence that the extremely hesitant policies adopted by the euro zone officials to deal with the Greek crisis caused it to spread further and have much stronger negative effects than was necessary. However, although not all-powerful, market reactions seem to have played a role in forcing governments to make policy adjustments more rapidly than they would have otherwise. Likewise, many have argued that the failure to bail out Lehman Brothers caused much greater contagion during the US subprime crisis than was necessary.[104]

The most common way of testing for international contagion has been to look for whether there are substantial increases in the correlations of the behavior of financial markets across countries.[105] This is consistent with the old adage that in crises the only things that go up are correlations. However, such testing does not allow us to tell how much of the contagion was unjustified, nor whether the increases in correlations were due largely to common shocks. Furthermore, the welfare effects of contagion may be affected much more by the size of the total fall of asset prices than by the level of their daily covariance once the crises have hit. The effects of movements in the prices of financial assets also can vary greatly. Thus, the contagions of currency crises are much more harmful if they are also associated with domestic banking and financial crises.

The major channels through which the effects of crises are spread are trade and capital flows and changes in perceptions and expectations. The latter are usually accompanied by changes in international capital flows, but the transmission may go beyond actual flows. Shocks will often change prices directly even before funds flow.

Crises may often generate "wake-up" calls which lead actors to reevaluate their perceptions of preexisting situations in other countries. The Asian crisis was an important example of this. Wake-up calls usually involve looking more closely for possible problems in other institutions and countries. They may also cause reevaluations of the types of narratives or mental

[104] For discussions and additional references to studies of this crisis, see Davies (2010), Lo (2012), and Willett (2012).

[105] Technically, correlations are not the best way to test for increased co-movements. More recent studies use more sophisticated statistical techniques and also look at the spread of clusters of greater volatility as well as co-movements of interest rates and asset prices. See, for example, the analysis and references in Bird et al. (2017), Forbes (2012), and Pericoli and Sbracia (2003). Some studies also look at the transmission of volatility. Bird et al. test the efficient market hypothesis with respect to the interest rates on Greek government debt during its crisis that substantial changes in market prices should only occur in the face of news. They find that a majority of the large moves were associated with news, but a substantial minority were not, supporting the view in this study that both efficient market and behavioral finance theory are important factors.

models that had been used to evaluate situations. For example, in the cases of both the Mexican and Asian crises in the 1990s, many investors had focused too heavily on the strong domestic macroeconomic fundamentals in these countries and paid too little attention to exchange rate overvaluation and financial sector problems.

When investors or borrowers suddenly discover that they had been using faulty analysis, it does not require irrational panic for them to react initially by pulling back on their investments. There may initially be a fairly general pullback which then becomes more focused as market actors have more time to evaluate the new situation. An example is the Mexican crisis of 1994–95 where there were widespread, though somewhat mild, effects across most of Latin America, but major crises hit only a few countries which had weak economic and financial fundamentals.

Of course, rational explanations for contagion should not be taken as strong evidence that no excessive reactions also occurred, Behavioral finance points to a number of factors that may lead markets to overreact. Panic and tendencies to follow the herd are prominent among them. Such rational explanations, however, do offer a valuable perspective that we should not assume that all of the contagion is irrational and should investigate to what extent it may have been due to fundamental factors.

Contagion based on fundamentals is often called interdependence to distinguish it from possible irrational contagion. For example, if a crisis leads to a recession, the country will import less, directly leading to declines in income for its trading partners. Real effects may also occur indirectly. The severe recessions associated with the Asian crisis led to a substantial fall in the demand for oil, and the resulting fall in prices was a major cause of the substantial fall in Russia's export proceeds. This was an important contributor to the Russian crisis in 1998. Consequently, the crisis in Asia is sometimes described as leading to rolling crises across the globe.[106] This is indeed true, but this spread was due primarily to interdependence rather than irrational contagion.

Kaminsky et al. (2003) make an important distinction between mild contagion, which they call "ripple effects," and major contagions, which they label "fast and furious." They find that the most important factors putting a country at risk of such contagion are large previous capital inflows, common leveraged lenders, and the initial crisis being largely a surprise. They also emphasize that most crises do not lead to fast and furious contagions, suggesting limits to how strongly the international financial system is subject to irrational panic.

[106] See, for example, Kindleberger and Aliber (2011).

Irrational contagion resulting from panic should occur quickly, so that crises that spread slowly are unlikely to be caused primarily by irrational reactions. This focus helps us realize that the Asian crisis was really two crises. The contagion from Thailand to Southeast Asia was fast and furious, but it was not until months later that major crises hit the Northeast Asian countries of Hong Kong, Korea, and Taiwan. There is little question that the crises in Southeast Asia made the later speculative attacks in Northeast Asia more likely, but it seems highly doubtful that they occurred primarily from unjustified panic.

The evaluation of the importance of irrational speculation can be particularly difficult in the case of the pullback of investments in countries not directly connected to crises. There is likely something to the argument that some investors viewed the East Asian economies as one investment bundle, and thus with the crisis in some Asian countries pulled back their investments in all of them, and of course this would be the case with regional Asian funds.

However, large losses in one market may quite rationally require portfolio reallocations and reductions in investments in other areas. Indeed, some risk management programs call for doing this automatically. This is particularly true when the initial investments were highly leveraged, as often occurs with international investments. Resulting margin calls stimulated by falling asset values may require reducing funds in a number of countries. Somewhat ironically, to minimize losses from forced sales in thin markets, these cutbacks are often concentrated in markets which were the most developed and liquid, giving the impression that irrational speculation was hitting countries with the strongest fundamentals.

In terms of second- and third-generation crisis models, such developments can be the event that tips countries with vulnerable fundamentals from good to bad equilibria, generating even greater capital outflows. And where high leverage is involved, all such investments are in the vulnerable zone, irrespective of the countries' economic fundamentals.

These considerations strengthen the case for official lenders of last resort. In closed economies, lender of last resort functions are the responsibility of national governments and central banks, but in open economies with large crises, countries may not have sufficient international reserves to keep outflows of capital from creating major currency depreciations that in turn will further worsen the balance sheets of many financial institutions. While not a true international lender of last resort, the IMF is the international institution which most closely serves that function. Emergency support from the IMF is often supplemented by bilateral arrangements, such as Federal Reserve swaps and regional financial arrangements.[107]

In such cases, the distinction between illiquidity and solvency can be important. Institutions with sound but longer-term investments and with insufficient short-term liquidity could be forced by a crisis to liquidate assets at fire sale prices, which can cause initially solvent enterprises to become insolvent. The concept of solvency is much more difficult to apply operationally to countries than to businesses, but the basic concept still applies. This implies that even countries with strong macroeconomic fundamentals may be in a vulnerable zone if their short-term liquid liabilities substantially exceed their international reserves and easy borrowing power. This is especially true where a high proportion of foreign debt is denominated in foreign currency. This was definitely a problem in the Asian crisis and led these countries to substantially build up their holdings of international reserves after the crisis.[108]

In summary, contagion may take many forms and is not always primarily associated with overreactions and irrational panic. Often the more serious market failures occurred before the crisis when various actors took on financial positions that were much riskier than they realized. In this process, behavioral factors such as faulty mental models or narratives, herding, hubris, and confirmation bias often played important roles. Often the contagion resulting from crises has a substantial rational component, and it is not unusual for behavioral factors to have been more important in the prelude to crisis than during the crisis itself. In a number of cases, such as Asia in the 1990s and Greece in the 2000s, substantial financial imbalances were generated by excessive capital inflows during good times. In each case, substantial inflows were justified by the fundamentals, but considerations such as overoptimism, insufficient homework, and the herding of narratives led the inflows be excessive, leading to bubbles in financial assets and real estate prices. In these cases, international financial markets acted as facilitators of financial crises, rather than as providers of discipline.

7.7 Implications for the Effectiveness of Official Intervention in the Foreign Exchange Markets

There has been considerable controversy about the effectiveness of official intervention policy in the foreign exchange markets. Most of the debate over

[107] The World Bank and regional development banks do sometimes help out as well, but their focus is on longer-term loans for development purposes.

[108] Such potential liquidity problems present a strong case for the IMF to have the power to operate as a quasi-international lender of last resort, and in the Asian crisis it played this role to some extent, but its methods of implementation attracted considerable criticism. In South Korea the Asian crisis is still often referred to as the IMF crisis. The IMF certainly behaved imperfectly during the crisis, but in my judgment not nearly as badly as some critics have argued.

this issue has focused on the effects of sterilized intervention. With sterilization, the effects of the changes in international reserves associated with the intervention are not allowed to affect the domestic money supply. If the interventions are not sterilized, then they will directly affect the domestic money supply since international reserves are a part of the monetary base. Such interventions are essentially an open market operation which is carried out in the foreign exchange market instead of the domestic money market. It is generally agreed that such monetary operations will affect the exchange rate. With respect to unsterilized intervention, the policy issue is the degree to which monetary policy should respond to domestic versus external developments.[109] Note that an important implication of the MF model is that with perfect capital mobility, effective sterilization is not possible.

The effectiveness of sterilized intervention has two different aspects. One is whether it will actually affect exchange rates. The second is whether, assuming that it can affect the exchange rate, the intervention improves welfare, such as by offsetting the effects of destabilizing or insufficiently stabilizing speculation.

Whether sterilized intervention can affect exchange rates has often been debated in terms of an unqualified yes or no. However, this is not a useful way to look at the question. But as is emphasized in behavioral finance, markets can behave differently in different situations and at different times. A more fruitful framing of the issue asks under what conditions can sterilized intervention affect the exchange rates and when not.

A foreign exchange market may be quite thin in some situations but quite thick in others. The size of capital movements can vary greatly depending on the degree of development of foreign exchange and domestic financial markets in different countries, the breadth and effectiveness of any capital controls, expectations and the amount of uncertainty. Even for the same country, the degree of capital mobility may vary a great deal from one situation to another.

Even for advanced economies with open capital markets, sterilized intervention can have an effect on exchange rates when speculative expectations are not strongly held, so that the arbitrage and speculative schedules are inelastic. This is particularly likely to happen when developments generate a great deal of uncertainty. In such cases rates may be forced away from equilibrium levels, not only by destabilizing speculation but also by a lack of stabilizing speculative funds. In such cases, sterilized intervention has the potential of improving efficiency.[110]

[109] A complex set of factors influence this issue, many of them highlighted in the theory of optimal currency areas. See the analysis and references in Dellas and Tavlas (2009) and Willett (2003).

[110] Of course, this does not mean that officials will always intervene in efficient ways. Indeed, there are many cases where interventions have generated moves away from rather than toward equilibrium.

At other times, capital mobility may be quite high and sometimes asymmetrical. Consider the case of a country with an exchange rate that the market views as being substantially overvalued. This is likely to lead to large outflows even for countries where the response of capital flows to changes in interest rates is usually fairly low. This is the classic case of not knowing whether there will be an exchange rate change in the near future, but knowing the direction of change if one does occur, the famous one-way speculative option. In such situations capital mobility may be quite low with respect to inflows responding to increased interest rates in the crisis country. In such cases, the main effect of the initial interventions is to allow some individuals to get their money out at the old exchange rate.

In the aftermath of major depreciations, the market may become thin for a while. Both the difference between short-term and longer-term elasticities of trade flows, and the possibility of initial excessive panic could lead exchange rates to initially over-depreciate, because of the great uncertainty, only a limited number of speculators are willing to take advantage of the resultant potential profit opportunities. This may have occurred with the exchange rate overshooting that developed for some countries during the Asian crisis. This is a case where greater sterilized intervention may have been both feasible and useful.

However, it may often be difficult in real time to know whether or not the market is pushing the exchange rate away from equilibrium. It is doubtful that officials will always have better estimates of equilibrium exchange rates than will private sector agents. And apart from such technical issues, government officials may have exchange rate objectives other than promoting exchange rate equilibrium. Many of the kinds of biases that we have discussed with respect to financial sector actors can also apply to government officials. Such biases may lead officials to assume that any market pressures that move rates away from their objectives must be destabilizing, an example of wishful thinking, allowing normative objectives to influence their positive views. Considerable uncertainty and short time horizons can add to these tendencies since one can be sure of the costs of taking actions now, but the future crisis may not happen, at least not until later.[111] And confirmation bias may lead officials to be slow in giving appropriate weight to any evidence suggesting that their assumptions that there was destabilizing speculation were not correct.

These are not just theoretical possibilities. Thus, sadly, it is not unusual to face situations where we must trade off between imperfect markets and imperfect governments.[112]

[111] See the discussion in Amri and Willett (2017).

[112] An example is the problem of regulatory capture where over time the regulators take on the perspective of the firms they are regulating and end up doing more to protect the firms in the

8 Concluding Remarks

While the efficient market approach provides us with many valuable insights, such as the important distinction between the effects of anticipated and unanticipated policies, assumptions sometimes lead to conclusions which don't just miss some details but are fundamentally misleading. Such views contributed importantly to the US subprime mortgage crisis. This problem is not limited to efficient market theory but applies to almost all theories of international monetary and financial behavior. These theories are typically highly appropriate for the analysis of some situations, but not for others. This Element provides numerous examples of this with respect to a wide range of popular theories.

While some advocates of behavioral economics and finance have launched full scale attacks on the traditional economists' assumptions of rational behavior and efficient markets, many others view the behavioral approach as a complement to these traditional assumptions. This is the view that I have adopted, while adding analysis of several other approaches, such as evolutionary and complexity economics.

My approach to analyzing cases of market malfunctions is to begin by looking at whether they can be adequately explained by factors such as perverse incentive structures or situations of considerable complexity and uncertainty. Where such factors do not seem to offer sufficient explanations, I go into my toolbox and consider various behavioral factors. In the many cases I have studied, pure behavioral factors on their own seldom are sufficient explanations. However, when combined with the effects of uncertainty and rational incentives they often offer considerable explanatory power. For example, major asset bubbles rarely begin purely from psychological factors, but they can be quite important in causing price increases to go much too far. Likewise, the sparks that generate currency and financial crises, asset market crashes, or capital flow reversals are seldom purely shifts from optimism to pessimism among market participants.

Behavioral biases tend to be much more prevalent under conditions of great uncertainty, and there are often important interactions among biases which can multiply their effects.

For example, in addition to rational incentives for herding, the desire to be a member of a group, overoptimism, hubris, and FOMO can be important.

industry than looking out for the consumer, which was the original purpose of the regulation. The transportation industry in the US is a famous example. Another example is that the legitimate objective of protecting key industries from foreign competition for national security reasons is often used as a justification for protecting industries that have political clout but are not really essential for national security.

Furthermore, confirmation bias and hesitancy to admit that one is wrong can blunt the warning signals that the herd is going in the wrong direction.

This Element also emphasizes the importance of the narratives or mental models that guide behavior, and argues that faulty mental models are often major causes of market excesses and currency and financial crises. Contrary to what is frequently thought, these various biases and faulty mental models are more important causes of the buildup of financial imbalances precrisis, than of excessive market reactions during crises. This has the important implication that international financial markets are often facilitators of the buildups of financial imbalances rather than offering early warning signals and acting as sources of discipline. The Greek crisis in the 2000s is an important illustration. Consistent with the MF model based on static expectations, large capital inflows helped finance the Greek fiscal deficits for years and kept interest rates from rising. To act as sources of discipline, markets need to be well informed and operate on the basis of expectations that are largely rational.

The types of biases discussed here are by no means limited to the behavior of the private sector. They can also contribute importantly to perverse government policies. For example, wishful thinking and confirmation biases can cause governments to postpone taking needed policy adjustments until the continuing imbalances lead to currency and financial crises. And the adoption of faulty mental models, such as the idea that tax cuts will usually reduce rather than increase fiscal deficits, or that cutting interest rates is the best way to fight inflation, can contribute importantly to the creation of crises such as those that hit the UK and Turkey in recent years.

The possibility of the existence of limits to arbitrage is a key component of behavioral finance and has a number of important implications for international monetary and financial analysis. Particularly important is that while international capital mobility is often quite high, this does not imply that it is usually close to perfect as is assumed in many models. Nor are capital controls the only cause of imperfect capital mobility. Therefore, more attention needs to be paid to the implications of imperfect capital mobility and to the factors that help explain it. Under such conditions, sterilized intervention in the foreign exchange can at times become effective and the international monetary trilemma need not always hold in the short run.

An important conclusion is that for a number of reasons markets may behave differently under different conditions. For example, when there is great uncertainty and the foreign exchange markets are quite thin, then sterilized intervention may have substantial effects on market rates, while intervention in hopes of maintaining a substantially overvalued exchange rate will more often be futile, only serving to delay an inevitable devaluation.

The latter type of case illustrates that many of the types of biases that may impede the efficient operation of private markets can also significantly affect the actions of government and monetary officials. Political considerations in the face of time inconsistency problems can provide rational reasons for officials to delay needed balance of payments adjustments for too long, since the costs come largely up front and are highly visible while the benefits of avoiding a crisis come later and aren't so visible. The types of psychological biases that can contribute to asset market bubbles can also lead to wishful thinking by officials, which strengthens their tendencies to postpone needed adjustments. The world is uncertain and new developments might make the problem go away. In such cases, the normative desire for this to be true may color positive analysis of the probability that this will in fact occur.

Another important implication is that behavioral causes of market failures are often more important in contributing to the development of capital flow surges and asset market booms that go too far, than to the market reactions to crises once they break out. As is shown in the literature on far-from-equilibrium behavior, in such cases a small shock can have large consequences. While in many cases there are undoubtedly some excessive market reactions, much of the contagion following crises may be quite rational, with the initial crisis leading to wake-up calls which lead market participants to realize that they had taken on much riskier positions than they had realized. The Asian crisis in the 1990s and the euro crisis in the 2000s are important examples.

A frequent criticism of the behavioral approach is that it does not provide a general theory like the efficient markets hypothesis and is instead merely a collection of different types of behavior. However, this is true also of mainstream international monetary, macro, and financial models. There are none which are capable of analyzing all types of questions and situations correctly. The world is complex and filled with uncertainties, and behavior is often different in different situations. Thus, thinking that any one theory or approach is all one needs to know has attractions but is highly dangerous. I hope that this Element has convincingly shown how valuable the insights we can get from paying attention to a number of different approaches can be.

Recognizing that a number of different theories can be relevant and that their relative importance can vary from one situation to another need not lead to the pessimist conclusion that anything can happen. A good, applied theorist needs to develop a sense of what theories, approaches, or combinations of them are most appropriate to different situations. In other words, one must practice contingent analysis. For example, new classical macroeconomics is usually more useful for longer term than short run analysis, and like most traditional Keynesian analysis the MF model is more applicable to the short run than the long run. In other words, the focus should be on the contingent analysis of what theories to use when.

Of course, no one can hope to do this perfectly nor be familiar with all of the different theories or approaches that may be relevant to a particular situation or question. What we can do, however, is to be aware of a number of different approaches and be willing to learn or consult with others where approaches that one has not mastered look like they may be relevant. We should try to keep open minds and, as Keynes and a number of other distinguished economists have advised us, we should be humble.

References

Acemoglu, D. and Restrepo, P. (2017). Secular stagnation? The effect of aging on economic growth in the age of automation. *American Economic Review*, 107(5), 174–179.

Albagli, E., Ceballos, L., Claro, S. and Romero, D. (2024). UIP deviations: Insights from event studies. *Journal of International Economics*, 148, 103877.

Allen, F., Babus, A. and Carletti, E. (2009). Financial crises: Theory and evidence. *Annual Review of Financial Economics*, 1(1), 97–116.

Amri, P. D. and Willett, T. D. (2017). Policy inconsistencies and the political economy of currency crisis. *Journal of International Commerce, Economics and Policy*, 08(1), 1750004.

Angkinand, A. P., Chiu, E. M. and Willett, T. D. (2009). Testing the unstable middle and two corners hypotheses about exchange rate regimes. *Open Economies Review*, 20, 61–83.

Angkinand, A. P., Sawangngoenyuang, W. and Wihlborg, C. (2010). Financial liberalization and banking crises: A cross-country analysis. *International Review of Finance*, 10(2), 263–292.

Auerbach, A. J. (2018). Measuring the effects of corporate tax cuts. *Journal of Economic Perspectives*, 32(4), 97–120.

Backhouse, R. E. and Boianovsky, M. (2016). Secular stagnation: The history of a macroeconomic heresy. *The European Journal of the History of Economic Thought*, 23(6), 946–970.

Barberis, N. and Thaler, R. (2002). *A Survey of Behavioral Finance*. NBER Working Paper No. 9222.

Beinhocker, E. (2007). Origin of Wealth: Evolution, Complexity, and the Radical Remarking of Economics. Harvard Business Review Press.

Bernstein, W. J. (2021). The Delusions of Crowds: Why People Go Mad in Groups. Grove Atlantic.

Bhoj, J. (2019). A study of origin and history of behavioral finance. *EPRA International Journal of Research and Development*, 4(11), 144–155.

Bird, G. (2016). Towards a better understanding of international capital volatility. *World Economics*, 17(3), 1–24.

Bird, G. (2018). Trumponomics and taxation. *World Economics*, 18(1), 173–191.

Bird, G., Du, W. and Willett, T. D. (2017). Behavioral finance and efficient markets: What does the euro crisis tell us? *Open Economies Review*, 28(2), 273–295.

Bird, G. and Willett, T. D. (2008). Why do governments delay devaluation? *World Economics*, 9(2), 55–74.

Bookstaber, R. (2007). A Demon of Our Own Design: Markets, Hegde Funds, and the Perils of Financial Innovation. John Wiley and Sons.

Bookstaber, R. (2017). The End of Theory: Financial Crises, the Failure of Economics, and the Sweep of Human Interaction. Princeton University Press.

Borio, C., James, H. and Shin, H. S. (2014, August). *The International Monetary and Financial System*. BIS Working Papers No. 457.

Bossaerts, P. (2009). What decision neuroscience teaches us about financial decision making. *Annual Review of Financial Economics*, 1(1), 383–402.

Brunnermeier, M. and Reis, R. (2023). A Crash Course on Crises: Macroeconomic Concepts for Run-ups, Collapses, and Recoveries. Princeton University Press.

Burnham, T. (2008). Mean Markets and Lizard Brains: How to Profit from the New Science of Irrationality. John Wiley and Sons.

Burton, E. T. and Shah, S. N. (2013). Behavioral Finance: Understanding the Social, Cognitive, and Economic Debates. John Wiley and Sons.

Chodorow-Reich, G., Zidar, O. and Zwick, E. (2024). Lessons from the biggest business tax cut in US history. *Journal of Economic Perspectives*, 38(3), 61–88.

Davies, H. (2010). The Financial Crisis: Who Is to Blame? Polity Press.

De Grauwe, P. and Grimaldi, M. (2006). The Exchange Rate in a Behavioral Finance Framework. Princeton University Press.

De Grauwe, P. and Ji, Y. (2019). Behavioral Macroeconomics: Theory and Policy. Oxford University Press.

Dellas, H. and Tavlas, G. S. (2009). An optimum-currency-area odyssey. *Journal of International Money and Finance*, 28(7), 1117–1137.

Dornbusch, R. (1976). Expectations and exchange rate dynamics. *Journal of Political Economy*, 84(6), 1161–1176.

Efremidze, L., Kim, S., Sula, O. and Willett, T. D. (2017). The relationships among capital flow surges, reversals and sudden stops. *Journal of Financial Economic Policy*, 9(4), 393–413.

Efremidze, L., Rutledge, J. and Willett, T. D. (2016). Capital flow surges as bubbles: Behavioral finance and McKinnon's over-borrowing syndrome extended. *The Singapore Economic Review*, 61(2), 1640023.

Fisher, I. (1930). The Theory of Interest as Determined by Impatience to Spend Income and Opportunity to Spend It. Macmillan.

Forbes, K. (2012). *The "Big C": Identifying and Mitigating Contagion. Kansas City Fed Jackson Hold Conference*. NBER Working Paper No. 18465.

Friedman, M. (1953). *The Case for Flexible Exchange Rates*. Essays in Positive Economics. University of Chicago Press. pp. 157–203.

Friedman, M. (1957). A Theory of the Consumption Function. Princeton University Press.

Gennaioli, N. and Shleifer, A. (2018). A Crisis of Beliefs: Investor Psychology and Financial Fragility. Princeton University Press.

Ghosh, A. R., Ostry, J. D. and Qureshi, M. S. (2019). Taming the Tide of Capital Flows. The MIT Press.

Greenspan, A. (2014). The Map and the Territory 2.0: Risk, Human Nature, and the Future of Forecasting. Penguin Books.

Hannan, S. A. (2018). Revisiting the Determinants of Capital Flows to Emerging Markets–A Survey of the Evolving Literature. International Monetary Fund.

Hansen, A. H. (1953). A Guide to Keynes. McGraw-Hill.

Hassan Almahmood, H., Al Munyif, F. and Willett, T. (2018). Most Speculative Attacks. *Journal of International Commerce, Economics, and Policy*, 9(1),1–9.

Ibbotson, R. G., Idzorek, T. M., Kaplan, P. D. and Xiong, J. X. (2018). Popularity: A Bridge between Classical and Behavioral Finance. CFA Institute Research Foundation.

Illiashenko, P. (2017). *Behavioral Finance: History and Foundations*. Visnyk of the National Bank of Ukraine, (239), pp. 28–54.

Kahneman, D. (2011). Thinking, Fast and Slow. Farrar, Straus and Giroux.

Kalemli-Özcan, Ș. and Varela, L. (2021). *Five Facts about the UIP Premium* (No. w28923). National Bureau of Economic Research.

Kaminsky, G. L., Reinhart, C. M. and Vegh, C. A. (2003). The unholy trinity of financial contagion. *Journal of Economic Perspectives*, 17(4), 51–74.

Kay, J. and King, M. (2020). Radical Uncertainty: Decision-Making beyond the Numbers. W. W. Norton.

Keynes, J. M. (1921). A Treatise on Probability. Macmillan.

Kern, A., Reinsberg, B. and Rau-Göhring, M. (2019). IMF conditionality and central bank independence. *European Journal of Political Economy*, 59, 212–229.

Kindleberger, C. P. and Aliber, R. (2011). Manias, Panics, and Crashes: A History of Financial Crises, 6th ed. Basic Books.

King, M. (2016). The End of Alchemy: Money, Banking, and the Future of the Global Economy. W. W. Norton.

Knight, F. H. (1921). Risk, Uncertainty and Profit. Hart, Schaffner and Marx.

Krugman, P. (1979). A model of balance-of-payments crises. *Journal of Money, Credit and Banking*, 11(3), 311–325.

Krugman, P. (1996). *Are Currency Crises Self-Fulfilling?* NBER Macroeconomics Annual.

Lo, A. W. (2012). Reading about the financial crisis: A twenty-one-book review. *Journal of Economic Literature*, 50(1), 151–178.

Lo, A. W. (2019). Adaptive Markets: Financial Evolution at the Speed of Thought. Princeton University Press.

Lucas, R. E. and Sargent, T. J. (1978)(1997). After Keynesian Macroeconomics. After the Phillips Curve: Persistence of High Inflation and High Unemployment, (1978), pp. 49–72. In *A Macroeconomics Reader* (pp. 282-306). Routledge.

Malkiel, B. G. (2023). A Random Walk down Wall Street. W. W. Norton.

Menschel, R. (2002). Markets, Mobs and Mayhem: How to Profit from the Madness of Crowds. John Wiley and Sons.

Minsky, H. (1975). John Maynard Keynes. Colombia University Press.

Minsky, H. (1986). Stabilizing an Unstable Economy. McGraw Hill.

Morris, S. and Shin, H. (1998). Unique equilibrium in a model of self-fulfilling currency attacks. *American Economic Review*, 88(3), 587–597.

Obstfeld, M. and Rogoff, K. (1996). Foundations of International Macroeconomics. MIT Press.

Obstfeld, M. and Rogoff, K. (2000). *The Six Major Puzzles in International Macroeconomics: Is There a Common Cause?* NBER Macroeconomics Annual.

Obstfeld, M. and Taylor, A. M. (2017). International monetary relations: Taking finance seriously. *Journal of Economic Perspectives*, 31(3), 3–28.

Pericoli, M. and Sbracia, M. (2003). A primer on financial contagion. *Journal of Economic Surveys*, 17(4), 571–608.

Perlmutter, S., Campbell, J. and MacCoun, R. (2024). Third Millennium Thinking: Creating Sense in a World of Nonsense. Little, Brown Spark.

Pilbeam, K. (2023). International Finance. Bloomsbury Publishing.

Pinker, S. (2021). Rationality: What Is It, Why It Seems Scarce, Why It Matters. Viking.

Rajan, R. (2001). The (Ir)relevance of currency crisis theory to the devaluation and collapse of the Thai Baht. *Princeton Studies in International Economics*, No.88, February.

Rey, H. (2013). *Dilemma not Trilemma*. Paper presented at Kansas City Fed Economic Policy Conference.

Schuknecht, L. (2022). Debt Sustainability: A Global Perspective. Cambridge University Press.

Sharma, R. (2024). What Went Wrong with Capitalism. Simon and Schuster.

Shiller, R. J. (2020). Narrative Economics: How Stories Go Viral and Drive Major Economic Events. Princeton University Press.

Shleifer, A. (2000). Inefficient Markets: An Introduction to Behavioral Finance. Oxford University Press.

Simon, H. (1991). Bounded rationality and organizational learning. *Organization Science*, 2(1), 125–134.

Smith, A. (1776). An Inquiry into the Nature and Causes of the Wealth of Nations, In Edwin A. Seligman, ed., J. M. Dent, 1901. Vol. 1. W. Strahan; and T. Cadell.

Smith, V. (2008). Rationality in Economics: Constructivist and Ecological Forms. Cambridge University Press.

Summers, L. (2013). Why stagnation might prove to be the new normal. *Financial Times*, 15(12), 442.

Tavlas, G. S. (2024). The case for flexible exchange rates in 1953 and 1969: Friedman versus Johnson. *Journal of Money, Credit and Banking*. Volume 0, No. 0 (April 2024) pp. 1-28 https://onlinelibrary-wiley-com.ccl.idm.oclc.org /doi/pdf/10.1111/jmcb.13151.

Thaler, R. (2015). Misbehaving: The Marking of Behavioral Economics. W. W. Norton.

White, L. (1989). Competition and Currency: Essays on Free Banking and Money. New York University Press.

Walter, S. and Willett, T. D. (2012). Delaying the inevitable: A political economy approach to currency defenses and depreciation. *Review of International Political Economy*, 19(1), 114–139.

Willett, T. D. (1977). *Floating Exchange Rates and International Monetary Reform*. Books. Volume 172 of AEI studies, American Enterprise Institute for Public Policy Research. 146 pages.

Willett, T. D. (1988). Political Business Cycles: The Political Economy of Money, Inflation, and Unemployment. Duke University Press.

Willett, T. D. (2012). The role of defective mental models in generating the globe financial crisis. *Journal of Financial Economic Policy*, 4(1), 41–57.

Willett, T. D. (2022). New developments in financial economics. *Journal of Financial Economic Policy*, 14(4), 429–467.

Willett, T. D. (2024). Some implications of behavioral finance for international monetary analysis. *The Economic and Business Review*, 10(1), 7–29.

Willett, T. D., Almahmood, H. and Al Munif, M. (2018). Most speculative attacks don't succeed: Currency crises, and currency crashes. *Journal of International Commerce, Economic and Policy*, 9(1),1–9.

Willett, T. D. and Bird, G. (2008). Why do governments delay devaluation? *World Economics*, 9(2), 55–74.

Willett, T. D. and Bird, G. (2024). A tale of two trilemmas: Comparing the international monetary and financial trilemmas. *Journal of International Commerce, Economics, and Policy.* 15 (2), 2450007.

Willett, T. D., Bird, G. and Du, W. (2017). Behavioral finance and efficient markets: What does the euro crisis tell us? *Open Economies Review*, 28(2), 273–295.

Willett, T. D., Bird, G., Du, W. and Pentecost, E. (2017). Was it different the second time around? An empirical analysis of contagion during the crisis in Greece 2009–2015. *The World Economy*, 40, 2530–2540.

Willett, T. D., Chiu, E. and Walter, S. (2014). Fixed exchange rates and financial markets as sources of macroeconomic discipline. In T. Oatley, ed., Handbook of the International Political Economy of Monetary Relations. Edward Elgar Publishing, pp. 285–303.

Willett, T. D. and Forte, F. (1969). Interest rate policy and external balance. *The Quarterly Journal of Economics*, 83(2), 242–262.

Willett, T. D., Keil, M. W. and Ahn, Y. S. (2002). Capital mobility for developing countries may not be so high. *Journal of Development Economics*, 68(2), 421–434.

Willett, T. D., Nitithanprapas, E., Nitithanprapas, I. and Rongala, S. (2004). The Asian crises reexamined. *Asian Economic Papers*, 3(3), 32–87.

Willett, T. D., Salvatore, D. and Dean, J. W. (2003). The Dollarization Debate. Oxford University Press.

Willett, T. D. and Walter, S. (2012). Delaying the inevitable: A political economy approach to currency defenses and depreciation. *Review of International Political Economy*, 19(1), 114–139.

Willett, T. D. and Xue, S. (2024). The monetary trilemma need not hold in the short run: The case of Hong Kong. *Journal of International Commerce, Economics and Policy*, 15 (3), 2450018.

Zweig, J. (2007). Your Money and Your Brain: How the New Science of Neuroeconomics Can Help Make You Rich. Simon and Schuster.

Cambridge Elements

International Economics

Kenneth A. Reinert
George Mason University

Kenneth A. Reinert is Professor of Public Policy in the Schar School of Policy and Government at George Mason University where he directs the Global Commerce and Policy master's degree program. He is author of *An Introduction to International Economics: New Perspectives on the World Economy* with Cambridge University Press and coauthor of *Globalization for Development: Meeting New Challenges* with Oxford University Press. He is also editor of *The Handbook of Globalisation and Development* with Edward Elgar and co-editor of the two-volume *Princeton Encyclopedia of the World Economy* with Princeton University Press.

About the Series

International economics is a distinct field with both fundamental theoretical insights and increasing empirical and policy relevance. The *Cambridge Elements in International Economics* showcases this field, covering the subfields of international trade, international money and finance, and international production, and featuring both established researchers and new contributors from all parts of the world. It aims for a level of theoretical discourse slightly above that of the *Journal of Economic Perspectives* to maintain accessibility. It extends Cambridge University Press' established reputation in international economics into the new, digital format of *Cambridge Elements*. It attempts to fill the niche once occupied by the *Princeton Essays in International Finance*, a series that no longer exists.

There is a great deal of important work that takes place in international economics that is set out in highly theoretical and mathematical terms. This new Elements does not eschew this work but seeks a broader audience that includes academic economists and researchers, including those working in international organizations, such as the World Bank, the International Monetary Fund, and the Organization for Economic Cooperation and Development.

Cambridge Elements

International Economics

Elements in the Series

Debt Sustainability: A Global Perspective
Ludger Schuknecht

The RMB in the Global Economy
Yin-Wong Cheung

Export Quality and Income Distribution
Rajat Acharyya and Shrimoyee Ganguly

The East Asian Electronics Sector: The Roles of Exchange Rates, Technology Transfer, and Global Value Chains
Willem Thorbecke

Virtual Trade in a Changing World: Comparative Advantage, Growth and Inequality
Sugata Marjit, Gouranga G. Das and Biswajit Mandal

International Investment Income
Joseph P. Joyce

How the Brady Plan Delivered on Debt Relief: Lessons and Implications
Neil Shenai, Marijn A. Bolhuis

A Behavioral Finance Approach to International Monetary and Financial Analysis: Implications and Evidence
Thomas D. Willett

A full series listing is available at: www.cambridge.org/CEIE

Printed in the United Kingdom by TJ Clays Ltd.